D1306868

THE SWORD
and
WOMANKIND

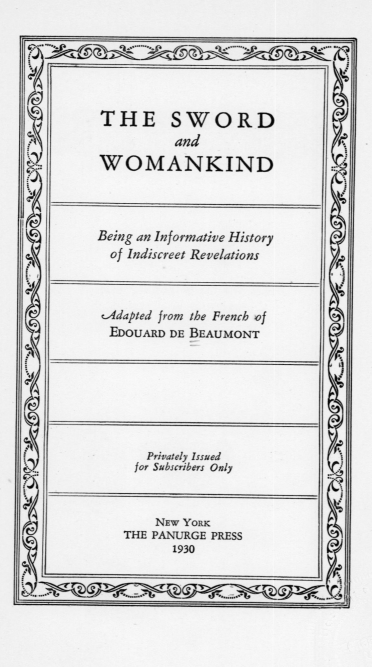

THE SWORD
and
WOMANKIND

*Being an Informative History
of Indiscreet Revelations*

Adapted from the French of
EDOUARD DE BEAUMONT

*Privately Issued
for Subscribers Only*

NEW YORK
THE PANURGE PRESS
1930

Printed in the United States of America

FOREWORD

To the Editors of The Panurge Press:

You ask me to write a few words of intro-duction to this first American edition of Edouard de Beaumont's "Sword and Womankind"*. I regret that I find it impossible because I disagree entirely with the writer and his subject. Beau-mont, with characteristic French point of view, believed in a feminine interpretation of history— which is, that all important historic events are caused by women. But unlike most Frenchmen he believed that all such events are caused by naughty women.†

Yet, though his point of view is exaggerated to the extreme, his book should be of special in-terest to us Americans who are taught the oppo-site extreme—which is almost as absurd. For

---

* L'EPEE ET LES FEMMES. *8vo. 1882. Paris: Librairie des Bibliophiles.*

† *Beaumont goes Pope one better. Pope, it may be remem-bered, says somewhere:*

"*Men, some to business, some to pleasure take;*
But every woman is at heart a rake."

the truth is, women have often determined the
destinies of nations, directed the rise and fall of
thrones. We can all imagine how the girl who
inspired the Love-Song of Solomon must have
also inspired him to great and lofty deeds,
though the facts are buried in forgotten lore.
And for every Joan La Romée or Sofia Perov-
skaia there have been dozens of royal mistresses
and celebrated courtesans who have been destructive forces of the worst.

The earliest of historians gave woman her
true place. He knew that if man falls to the
depths through woman it is through her too that
he rises to the heights. In the Garden of Eden
it was the woman who tempted the man and
brought them both to quick irremedial ruin. But
it was Eve also who offered Adam the forbidden
Fruit of the Tree of Knowledge, thus enabling
him to attain to the Godhead. Legend, fiction
or allegory, there is a symbolic truth behind it
that makes it one of the stories of the world.

Beaumont's idea is a simple one and can be
stated briefly in his own words. "The Sword
and Womankind," he declared, "are the rela-
tions between War and Love, between Mars
and Venus. I show how the Sword (i.e., War)
exercised an invigorating influence on women
during the Middle Ages. I then show how

women, by slow degrees from century to century, corrupted and eventually ruined their benefactor; how at the very epoch when women were all powerful and idolized as divinities, they broke down the heroic spirit and the ideal of chivalry; how grown weary of homage and respect, they gradually degraded Love, enforcing upon it the manners of gallantry and libertinism, voluntarily accepting the role of mere wantons . . . .

"I denounce fair ladies as responsible for the vices and extravagance of the young men at Camp and Court. I have made a point in my denunciations of carefully enumerating the various stratagems employed by women to attain their ends—to win free license for their adulterous excesses. I note from an accumulation of convincing proofs the sensual causes of the rapid degeneration of soldiers and men of rank and point out each step of their physical and moral decadence. . . ."

This argument of Beaumont does not appear one whit as extravagant in outline as it appears on a perusal of his book. For he brings forward only such facts as will prove his thesis* and often

---

* One instance out of many. Beaumont quotes from Dr. Johannes Scherr's "Society and Manners in Germany" again and again, though the book is as untrustworthy as a person on the witness stand.

refers to sources of a highly questionable na-ture. Besides, he is forever generalizing from individual, isolated cases which sometimes leads, as Othello said, to the most lame and impotent conclusions. As a woman-hater Beaumont makes Ecclesiastes and Schopenhauer look like novices. But Ecclesiastes and Schopenhauer were great men and if they wore blinkers where women were concerned, they at least judged men impartially and saw the facts of life with a clearness of vision seldom surpassed. Whereas Beaumont offers you nothing to compensate for his extraordinary misogynism, nothing save his multitudinous documentation of interesting an-ecdotes about women and their frank, challeng-ing misbehavior. This, however, justifies his book, particularly to Americans, for we know next to nothing about the erotic masterpieces of literature.*

Nor is Beaumont's misogynism his worst fault. There are others, more grievous, more glaring, which I shall pass over in silence. After all, a novel is judged by its characters mainly, an

---

* *Hardly one educated American in ten thousand has read a dozen such classics. With the exception of the "Arabian Nights," the "Memoirs of Jacques Casanova," Balzac's "Droll Stories," Rabelais, Boccaccio's "Decameron," the "Perfumed Garden" and perhaps "Fanny Hill," Americans are astonish-ingly ignorant of this forbidden field of literature.*

essay by its writer's brains, a history by its sense of proportion as well as by its interpretation of events.* Beaumont's book aims to be a history and its sense of values is as faulty as its interpretation of facts.

"The Sword and Womankind" inevitably reminds me of Richard Burton's "Book of the Sword."† But what a difference! Burton's book is even more documented than Beaumont's. It is full of footnotes, anthropological, historical, religious—indeed, like many another Burton book, the footnotes are the best part of the story.

---

* Few haphazard critics realize this. A novel is usually judged by its plot which is why even able readers see little or nothing in Joyce's "Ulysses." Yet Rabelais and Cervantes should have taught us the truth long ago. When the first volume of Frank Harris's autobiography appeared, Bernard Shaw wrote the author that he could have defended the book had it not been for the photographic illustrations of pretty, naked girls. One might as well condemn a painting because of its frame.

† Like Burton, Beaumont was an excellent swordsman and an authority on ancient arms. Otherwise the men were as different as chalk from cheese. Burton, a Titan of heroic mould, was a world-adventurer, a master of men and languages, with an extraordinary passion for the curious by-paths of human behavior. Beaumont, on the other hand, wasted the best part of his life on second-rate painting.

Incidentally it may be worth noting that "The Book of the Sword" is utterly unknown in the United States. Not without reason, for in the same country Fitzgerald's "Rubaiyat of Omar Khayyam" is read by a thousand persons for every one who reads Burton's far greater "Kasidah."

If there are frequent dull gaps in the "Book of the Sword," due to the highly technical nature of the subject and its treatment of pre-Renaissance times, one is constantly rewarded by tidbits of strange, esoteric information sprinkled throughout the volume. While this is also true of Beaumont's book, there is a stimulating power in Burton, arising from his personal experience and observation, which is entirely lacking in the former. For Beaumont hadn't a tithe of Burton's brains or critical insight, and wrote at second-hand and consequently tried to prove a thesis which can seem plausible only to a misogynist.*

I have already said that, for all its faults, Beaumont's book is of special value to us Americans who know so little of women, although the liberation of woman has been our chiefest contribution to the modern world.

Even more than our architecture, even more than our introduction of science and the machine into the daily lives of men, ought we to be

---

* *Edouard Charles de Beaumont, born in Lannion, 1819, died in Paris, 1888, was a French painter, lithographer and fencing-master. His paintings, principally in genre, are very delicate and spirituel. He was one of the founders of the Society of French Water-Color Painters, contributed numerous magazine articles, wrote several books none of which has been translated into English except "The Sword and Womankind."*

proud of our treatment of women. Think of England or France or Germany and compare their attitude to women with ours, and you must recognize at once how immeasurably more independent is the American type.

Yet in all our literature we have produced only one man who knew and painted women profoundly, only one man who has enlarged our conception of womanhood. Of course, here and there an American has done a superb portrait but these half dozen or less have been more the results of chance than indicative of deep understanding.

And when we do get a few studies of women, usually harmless, trivial novels by tenth-rate American novelists, they are immediately suppressed in one section of the country or another. For what gets by in Chicago by no means gets by in New York, and what gets by in New York by no means gets by in Boston. Thanks to the war we have today a gratuitous censorship of everything from the drama to drink. Naturally, our morals must be protected also in literary matters by censors with baby minds, though from the point of view of pornography ours is the purest of contemporary literatures.

There is a soul of goodness in things evil, as Shakespeare knew, and if the war has put back

*the hands of the clock in matters of personal lib-
erty and given us the twin evils of Prohibition
and Censorship, the thunder and lightning of
war have purified the air and left us forever
dissatisfied with our past literature which had
no relation to the realities of life.*

*Whatever one may think of the extreme bold-
ness of James Joyce's huge experiment,
"Ulysses," or Frank Harris's daring autobiography, "My Life," or D. H. Lawrence's extraordinary novel, "Lady Chatterley's Lover," no
one who knows these men and their earlier work
can question their desperate sincerity. To me
it is intensely significant that these three at-
tempts to break through the childish prudery of
our literature and bring it back to the virile days
when men wrote books for men, should have
been written in the first decade after the war.*

*In a thousand years, when almost all English
books written in the last decade shall have been
forgotten in the Ewigkeit, men will read these
books with gratitude for the quickening wisdom
that is in them. Joyce, Harris, Lawrence—
these will be names to conjure with though critics and censors today throw up their hands in
holy horror at their outspokenness. Sooner or
later every man who is worth his salt realizes the
joy of being utterly unafraid in speech and ac-*

tion. And ever thereafter censors to him are like fleas to a dog. . . .

A long way from such men to Beaumont, but even Beaumont is worth-while to some of us who recognize that every important literature save ours has a gallery of great women portraits. If we had more books like "The Sword and Womankind" we might read Brantome and Aretino and a dozen other similar writers, and thus grow to the realization that we Americans who have the most beautiful women in the world know least about the Eternal Feminine.

ESAR LEVINE

CONTENTS

xvi CONTENTS

THE SWORD
and
WOMANKIND

CHAPTER I

In Barbarous Ages Woman is a Divinity — Frea, the Scandinavian Venus

This history, being as it is the study of love and war from ancient times down to the year 1789, may for the present be subdivided under the following heads:

The influence of the Sword, taken as synonymous with War, Soldier and Gentleman, on the beauty and habits of women;

The influence of women on the vigor, fashions and destinies of the Sword;

And thirdly, the collective influence of these two activities, of Mars and Venus respectively, on the types of civilization which, especially on the feminine side, were successively *chivalrous, gallant, cavalier* and *libertine.*

The inquiry in question, starting from the strong, rude times of barbarism, when the warriors of those days treated women as a Divinity,* terminates at

---

* "They go so far as to believe that women possess a something divine and a faculty of throwing light on the future. Obediently following their advice, they look upon them as oracles. . . ."

"Under the Emperor Vespasian we saw a certain Velleda, who for a long period of time was held by the majority of persons to be a divinity. Before her, Aurinda and others

the end of the cowardly, petty period of false refinement that saw the Comtesse de Gacé, after a supper-
party, handed over naked to the will of lacqueys by
a company of dissolute men of rank.*

About the same period at which the mysterious
smiths of the North brought to highest perfection their
skill in the use of the hammer and anvil in tempering
steel, simultaneously the warriors of these Hyperborean
lands by their adoption of the sword as sole
weapon, assumed individually a distinct character as
men of the sword. They are the most complete representatives of the type we have to investigate, coming to
be identified with the Sword themselves.†

---

moreover won the same sort of veneration from the Nations."
—TACITUS, *Germania*, VIII.

"Velleda exercised from her retirement a power equal or
superior to that of kings. . . . The most famous warriors
dared enter on no enterprise without her assent, and consecrated to her a share of the booty,"—TACITUS, *Histories*,
V and VI.

* A practical joke of the same nature was played a
little later (in 1721) on Mme. de Saint-Sulpice, as related
by the avocat BARBIER in his *Journal.* "Some time since,"
he says, "the Comte de Charolois (after a supper-party of
debauchees) stripped her stark naked (she was dead drunk);
they then tied her up in a table-cloth with napkins, like a
child, and conveyed her in this condition in a coach to her
own door.

"Subsequently M. le Duc played her another fine trick.
They put two trains of powder with two (petards under her
seat. Her . . . is not burnt, but her belly is,—and a great
hole in her thigh to boot. It is said she will hardly recover.
La Peyronie, surgeon to the king, is attending her."

† In the Epic of the Nibelungenlied, *Sword* is synony-

Thus identified with his sword, burned on the pyre or buried along with it, his "iron bride,"* a thing of magic virtue is given talismanic names and strange or terrifying titles by the warrior; he calls it *Brimir* or *Gramr*, that is to say, *radiance* or *anguish*. Thenceforward in battle it is the act of individual daring that stands out conspicuously, a gauge of a man's forcefulness and vigor. On this foundation is built the spirit and degree of mutual respect of nations, and later on the hereditary aristocracy of valor. "Freya's sword is but ell-long"†—"How short soever your sword be, 'twill

---

mous with warrior. "The good sword Ortwin spake to the king."

Of old the warrior and his sword were inseparable. We see in the Laws of the Lombards that it was not lawful to take a man's sword in pledge.—*Leg. Longob.* Bk. I, tit. IX, Leg. XXXIII.—*Capitul.* Bk. IV, tit. II.

* "Yes, brave sword, I love three true, as though we were man and wife, as though thou wert my darling bride, hurrah!"—"Oh! heavenly embrace," replies the sword, "I wait with longing rapture for my groom. Come to me, my crown is for thee, hurrah!"—TH. KORNER, *Song of the Sword.*

In the laws of the Ripuarian Franks is found a recognized scale fixing the price of the different articles of a warrior's equipment in the time of Charlemagne:

A sword with sheath .... 7 sous
A sword without sheath............................ 3 —
A horse (entire), not blind, and sound 6 —

From which we see that a sword in those days cost more than a good horse.—DAVOUD-OGHLOU, *Histoire de la Législation des anciens Germains.*

† "Thor's hammer is short; the sword of Freya is but ell-long."—*Frithiof's Saga,* ch. XV.

never be too short," are primitive sayings of Icelandic proverbial wisdom, a motto as it were for the man of the Sword. Saxo Grammaticus has depicted his primordial and essential character in three words: *He fell, laughed loud and died.*

While noting the actual influence exercised in old days by War concurrently with the Sword over the feminine world of those times, we must recognize the fact that its activity in this direction is shown in its most manifest form among the Scandinavian peoples, whether Anglo-Saxon or Germanic. In those regions during the early epochs of history the Sword, in the literal acceptation of the word, altogether takes precedence over the spear.

Mediaeval documents hardly ever speak of any other weapon, so far as the north of ancient Europe is concerned, as the instrument of heroic prowess except keen-edged swords. "They cleave the bones of men's skulls," says a song of the heathen Anglo-Saxons. In another: "They have cloven the wall of the bucklers." —"We have fought out the fight with the sword," is the refrain recurring at almost every stanza in the Scandinavian poetry of Kraka; while Tacitus had already in his day mentioned the long swords of the Bretons.

The most ancient *Sagas* are far too modern to explain the primordial causes of the effects pointed out. Inquiry must needs be pushed back to yet remoter times.

In the cold countries of the North, home of those portentous blades and gigantic two-handed broad-swords* that were the shame and despair of later and weaker generations, Odin,† incarnation of the sword, god of the ravens of battle and of victory, the con-queror, the Northern Mars, who had come out of far off Asia with his band of warrior-priests, casts a first gleam of light along the course of legend that serves to reveal a second divinity,—the goddess of pallid sensu-alities. Through her, naturally enough, the wealth of generative power of the mighty wielders of the sword acts at first on the attributes and character of women.

The sword, robust and warlike engine, is their fit-ting mate; it passes on its own vigor to them, and thus, more surely than any magic girdles,‡ "hastens the birth of heroes." It forms the basis of a code of law, the *jus gladii*. At one time we shall find it rousing to the fray those formidable spinsters who in accordance with a custom prevalent among such savage peoples were bound, before being affianced to a husband, to have killed at least one enemy; at another time, creating the instincts of those redoubtable brides who, like the Nor-man dames in the time of William the Bastard, could

---

* The two-handed sword was *par excellence* a German, Swiss or Scotch weapon.

† Odin, Wodan or Wuotan.—Finne-Magnusen, *Vet. Boreal. Mithol. Lexicon,* under "Odin."

‡ OSSIAN's *Poems.* The girdle of strength and puissance was called *megingjar.*

not exist without caresses.* In those days it was an obligation on the noble and spirited creatures—from whom is descended the *weaker* sex, the sex that today affects an extremity of softness and gentleness!—to be, as for instance at Sparta, before all and above all, brave and strong.

To form an idea of this excessive superabundance of vigor and energy, the imagination must reproduce the barbarian life in all the vehemence of its activity, and picture the part played in it by the feminine element developed in these heroic proportions. Vigorous comrades of the sword, trusty companions in all the marches and expeditions of a wandering existence, they shared in the fight and animated the combatants with their songs and shrill outcries.

Broken to the endurance of cold and fatigue, without fixed home or habits of domesticity, wedded on the march under a wagon-tilt, how could they fail to be imbued with the very spirit and passions of war? Reared amid the crash and struggle of a life' of arms, they exhibited on occasion the frenzy of bacchantes. The women of the Teutons, and those of the Cimbri,† terrible in their passionate fury, could fight to the death,

---

* The wives of the Norman conquerors of England warned the latter by frequent messages that they could not any more remain faithful to their husbands or wait *any longer* for their return.

† "The women of the Cimbri armed themselves with swords, howling and grinding their teeth with fury and grief; they would strike Cimbri and Romans alike," etc.— PLUTARCH, *Life of Marius.*

and then, unable to survive defeat, would slay each other with the sword, or even strangle themselves in their long hair,—as they did at Aquæ Sextiae and at Vercellæ.

For these insatiable "mothers of the race," whose descendants, as depicted for us by Holbein and Albert Dürer, affected an intentional protuberance of the abdomen in walking,—precisely the opposite of the Greek Callipygé,—the Sword, the wedding-present a Teutonic bride* received to inculcate symbolically the duty of courage, was something more than a principle or law, more than a mere weapon; it was identified with man and his virility. The old *Degen* (sword) signified at one and the same time sword and warrior, just as in Spain the *Espada* of the bull-fights means the *Matador*.

Thus woman, in the northern half of Europe is found to have grown prolific, intrepid and vigorous under action of war. "They alone in the midst of disasters, these children of the giants, in other words, these daughters of the Sword, refuse to weep." Such is, in brief, the highest expression of their worth under purely martial influence.

On the side of physical perfection, their beauty, if not directly due to these conditions, was the result,—and especially so in Teutonic lands,—of various crossings of blood, an inevitable consequence of invasion

---

* *Et scutum cum framea gladioque* (and a buckler with javelin and sword).—TACITUS, *Germania*, XVIII.

and conquest, the vanquished mingling and uniting with the victors.

Thanks to this fusion, which later on will be further perpetuated by the wars and the *droits de seigneurs* of feudal times, fresh types of physiognomy are produced among the different peoples of Europe, particularly towards the North, yet without altering to any marked degree the fundamental character of each. The result-ing French composite type of Germain Pilon and the pink and white, full-breasted Hispano-Flemish of Ru-bens are for modern times the *fine flower* of this hap-hazard amalgamation due to the accidents of war alone,—to the action of the Sword under the varying forms its takes on the battle-field or in the boudoir.

Be this as it may, there is no doubt the crossing of races came about by means of slave-women or con-cubines, voluntary or involuntary subjects of the Sword, —which latter was more often than not polygamous. *They* were the first booty of victory, the first consola-tion after peril, and as ever with the soldier, the pastime of leisure moments in the interval of fighting.

In this way the courtesans of war helped to repair the ravages of slaughter and depopulation equally with the lawful mothers of families. Each played her own rôle, and each was capable, to judge from certain evi-dence from epochs not so very far removed in time, of bearing an average of a dozen children.* Of these the

---

* Queen Bertha had six children; Gerberga, nine; Ber-trada, five; Eleanor of Guienne, eleven; Marguerite of Pro-

males represented a sort of tribute women were under obligation to pay to their lord and master, the Sword.

This extreme fertility, stimulated as it was by the entirely muscular character of the life of those days, was mythologically under the auspices of Frea or Frigga,* the Eve, the Venus of Scandinavian peoples, Odin's mistress and goddess of repose and carnal plea-sure.

In virtue of this cult of Frea, in other words, the cult of the senses, the natural and healthy influence wielded by the sword over women is modified and supplemented by an exactly opposite influence. This constitutes the second part of the subject, to be next considered. It involves the examination of the influence successively exerted, in the north, over men of war by: 1. Love songs and their languishing strains; 2. Coarse sensuality on the women's part, and 3. Luxury borrowed by them from abroad.

At first commencement, as may be supposed, only

---

vence, eleven; Bonne of Luxembourg, nine; and Isabeau of Bavaria, twelve.

* Frea, Freia, Freya, Friga, Frey or Frikka, mistress of Odin, primitive woman, symbol of fecundity. Frea or Freia a synonym of love in the primitive Scandinavian tongue.

Frea is the chief of the goddesses, daughters of Fate and War, who number twelve in all; they are called Walky-ries, Gadur, Rosta and Skulda (the future), the youngest of the twelve Fairies. They go forth every day on horseback to choose the slain.—In Scandinavian mythology Folla is sister of Freia. Freia charmed arms, swords.

The Scandinavians had Frea's day, Freytag, Friday, in the same way as the Latin peoples had Venus' day.

simple means were employed to secure this domination of the flesh; but before very long a more complicated fabric of systematic allurement and cajolery was built up, in which every detail was directed to the one end, —success, a success the climatic conditions themselves favored. In ancient Germany, women, by the invention and application of ever fresh devices, undertook the task of taming and enfeebling the savage male, chaste originally by national character and now become by mere force of circumstances domestic and home-keeping.

The sentimental spirit, taking its first origin in the religion of Odin, named the inventor of songs,—at first nothing but annals of war and fighting,—is met with again in the very oldest traditions, in the mythical histories of noble families, where kings' sons are represented as wedding water-sprites,* and nymphs present warriors with the magic cup of enthusiasm.

The Sword, barbarous as it was in its origin, had yet from very early times its love-songs, destined little by little to supplant the war-songs. The Skalds, soldier-poets who, like the Bards, used to follow the armies, rousing with their voice the wild fierceness of the heroes, no doubt extolled in times of peace the merits and stalwart charms of the maids of the North.

The women of old Germany along with other daugh-

---

* "The son of the Swedish King Wilkinus was united with a goddess of the waters."—MALLET, *Introd. à l'Histoire de Danemark.*

ters of the North had encouraged from their earliest beginning these romantic *minnelieder*, which towards the seventh century took the place of the hymns of war and battle. They welcomed them from the very first as another weapon available in their system of gradual enfeeblement of their masculine companions.

Tacitus, with the intention of satirizing the vicious habits of his native Rome by making his description of Germany a sort of panegyric of barbarian manners and customs, says of the countless hordes of savage ruffians he then saw for the first time: "All they hold dear in the world they carry with them in their campaigns, and from the battle-field they can hear the shouts of their women. In them they possess spectators of the fray whose looks touch them most nearly and whose praises they most desire. . . . If they are hurt in their battles, they seek them out. Then without a sign of fear, the women count their injuries and hasten to suck the wounds."* They carried provisions to the fighting men and exhorted them to acquit themselves like men. "If they were victorious, they distributed among them praise and caresses. In this way women must never suppose themselves strangers to the sentiment of cour-age and the hazards of battle." This last phrase sums up the whole importance of female activity in its earlier stages of influence on men of the Sword.

---

* Justus Lipsius maintains they required, no doubt from motives of pride, that those they loved should not come back to them unwounded.

Allied at times politically against the Sword with
the pagan priests, who found in this conjunction at
once pleasure and profit, associated at a later period in
the mysteries rites of the soldier-priests of certain
orders, they are the subtle and insidious instruments of
their will. They give oracles, preside at certain sacri-
fices from which, it is said, men were strictly excluded,
and indulge in the strangest ceremonies. This is what
contemporary texts* tell us,—previous to the time
when they had occasion to expend their occult influence on furthering conversions to Christianity.

Even in the earliest and most primitive times of barbarism, deeply versed in wiles, they pose as mystic
agents of Nature's operations; they invent new superstitions; they become witches, prophetesses,† even
fairies. They rule the phases of the Moon, and it is supposed, can bewitch men's hearts‡ and tear them from

---

* POMPONIUS MELA, C. C. bk. III, ch. VIII; bk. IV, ch. IV.
JORNANDES, ch. XXIV.

† TACITUS, (Histories, IV.) says: "From time immemorial
the Germans have attributed to the majority of women the
power of knowing the future, and such as superstition gives
vogue to are looked upon as divinities."

‡ "Of the opinion held by many that certain women can
command the Moon and can drag the heart out of men,—
which is the belief of idolaters." List of superstitions and
pagan practices prevalent among the Franks, drawn up at the
Council of Leptines in 743 A.D. (Indiculus superstitionum
et paganiarum ad concilium Liptinense.)

In Scythia there were women whose look by itself bewitched men and caused their death.—PLINY, Natural Hist.,
Bk. VII.—SOLINUS, ch. VII.—AULUS GELLIUS, IX, ch. IV.

their bodies; they concoct love-philtres; they know magic words that will blunt steel; others again can charm swords,* and heal wounds. They are seen filling the part of doctors, "asking of the spirits to have their hands full of healing."†

By dint of such intrigues and every sort of clandestine manœuvre, all, however, directed to one and the same end, viz., the complete and final subjection of the Sword, little by little women make good their place among the elements of society, and always seconded by a system of organized cajolery that never rests, they become the undisputed masters of the heavy sleepers, princes of ignorance, whose beds and counsels they share, and who submit to this female domination, counting the days by the nights.‡

Finally brute force, or to speak more justly, heroic force, caught and imprisoned by the victorious activity of women, in which the love songs soon go from liberty to licence, expires like Attila on a woman's bosom.§

---

* "A fairy sharpened it. . . . She made the sign of the cross and bewitched it like a fairy as she was."—DEPPING, Wieland the Smith, ch. V. 45, and FRANCISQUE MICHEL, Recherches sur la fabrication des anciennes étoffes de soie, vol. I.

† The young Brunhild, learned in the runes, gives Sigurd strength and wisdom. She asks, by way of invocation, to have knowledge and "to have the hands full of healing." Song of the Edda.

‡ "Whereas we count by the days, they count by the nights."—TACITUS, Germania, XI.

§ "The King of the Huns (Attila) had just added to the number of his wives a maiden of an extraordinary beauty. Next morning in the nuptial chamber they found the girl

In this way in northern lands came about the first
degradation of the warrior and swordsman.

---

standing beside the unwounded corpse of Attila, weeping
beneath her veil.—Jornandes.

CHAPTER II

DEMORALIZATION OF WOMEN OF THE NORTH BY SOUTHERN LUXURY — GRADUAL DEGRADATION OF THE FEMININE IDEAL

It was by help of finery imported from Italy and across the Rhine and the Channel that in its third degree of development the influence of women made itself felt on the Sword.

From the moment of the first arrival of the Roman merchants and dealers, after the conquest, the Hyper- borean fair ones are dazzled, as savages would be, by the glittering tinsel of the South. To buy clothing of brilliant and startling hues, they sell for gold,—which they call *Freya's tears*,* that is to say, tears of Love,— their pale locks. These the Roman women of equivocal character, tired of black, yellow or golden hair, are eager to purchase. Note in this connection how it is especially on the feminine side that the ancient world shows itself most akin to the modern. From that time forth, warlike enthusiasm among women is a thing of the past: it is superseded by mere greed, leading as a

---

* The tears shed by the goddess of Love while searching for her husband were changed into gold; and the precious metal retained ever after the name of "Freya's tears."—OZA- NAM, *Les Germains avant le christianisme,* II.

natural consequence to fierce rapacity after loot. German and Frank women are mad after fine clothes and
jewels no less than the Gallic women Strabo tells of,
and luxury, a new and entrancing thing for them, en-
dows them with yet another new weapon of power.*
This is where their ascendancy was so dangerous, constraining the Sword to forget the wise precepts of older
days that discountenanced wealth as being a motive for
discord.

Women, from the very earliest period, gave their
favors to win the luxuries and refinements of dress, and
made it their business to seduce the fair-haired heroes,
who from Tacitus' day onwards, loved to remain virgin,† to dance naked amid swords, and in maturity con-
senting to marry but one wife. "Germany is chaste,"
is the burden of an old refrain. Meanwhile the viragos,

---

* The women of the North, as well as the Gaulish women
in the first ages of Christianity, soon rivaled the Roman
ladies in the luxury of their apparel. Commercial intercourse with the South brought to the further shores of the
Rhine cloth of gold, embroidered girdles, scented slippers,
for these coquettes of a new and still half-savage country,
and provided them with dyes to color their hair, naturally
of a too insipid blondeness, to the fashionable Roman tint.

† "With them it is held a disgrace to go with women before
the age of twenty, and they highly esteem such men as are
long without having a beard, because they suppose that in
this way they possess more strength and vigor. And indeed
this cannot be concealed, inasmuch as they bathe publicly
with the women in the rivers, and are clothed only in skins
which leave a great part of the body bare."—CAESAR, Commentaries, bk. IV, ch. II.

(specimens of whom quite of the ancient type, though a good deal toned down in the course of centuries, may still be met with at servants' hiring-fairs in country places), display their arms and bosoms bare.* Quaffing beer out of a human skull,† they essay by way of blandishments absurd affectations utterly incongruous with their massive proportions, taking the initiative in aggressions on the senses. It is easy to guess, taking into consideration the old-time prudery of the German men, what pains German women must have been at to so far seduce them and bring them by their allurements to become what they are.

There are sundry old German Masters, dating from the sixteenth century onwards, who exhibit the *Lans-quenets* and other fighting men of their country in full career down the tide of obscenity.

Thus was set up among the barbarians that civiliza-tion of feminine ruse and cunning which has produced a progressive hereditary enfeeblement of virile force, eventually bringing down to the short height of today the very lofty stature of the Hyperborean warriors.

Of course it must be understood that in virtue of their time-honored purity of morals this degenerative process was longer retarded, and by consequence more

---

* They wear no sleeves, and display besides their arms a portion of their bosom.

† On a feast day Rosamonda, wife of Alboin, king of the Lombards, in the sixth century, drank from the skull of her father-in-law.—PAUL DIACONUS, *Hist. Long.* See also HERODOTUS, IV.—STRABO, IV.—DIODORUS, V.

strikingly evident, when it did come, than anywhere
else in Europe. In the South, climate and primitive
character with its tendency to passion have from the
first been incompatible with so vigorous a development;
and accordingly in those countries the diminution of
human stature is much less obvious.

A very ancient Norwegian author, the Monk Theo-
dore,* fortifying himself by a passage from Pliny the
Elder, pronounces the dictum that the stature of mankind diminishes naturally in the course of ages.

This idea of gradual decrease is one of very ancient
antecedence, but merely going back half way in the past,
we find more than sufficient proofs to justify it.   These
proofs become especially noticeable after the first primitive savagery has been subjected on the sensual side to
some sort of discipline, when round the fighter's hearth
all the arts and allurements of the mistress of the house
were now combined to enervate him during his times of
leisure.

Tacitus has described the Germans as living in time
of peace in a sort of stolid indolence; and from his day
onwards far too much has been made by simple-minded
people of the domestic virtues of their descendants.

There it was in primitive times that round a rude
brazier in the long winters gathered a circle of drowsy
warriors;† then in later times, simultaneously with the

---

* *Commentarii historici duo* . . . by B. C. KIRCHMANN,
Amsterdam, 1684, I, 35.

† "Oh, King!" he said, "it is even as in winter time,
when you are seated at the feast with your great men and

adoption as a heraldic device of the two-headed eagle, women and beer exercised in the privacy of the interior their two-fold influence over these idolaters of "sentiment."

Such were the conditions of life amid which the mere swordsman, sitting absorbed in besotted dreams betwixt his huge, fat, carnal doxy and a row of beer-pots, waited for the highest offer of the recruiting officer and the most tempting chance of booty.

All commanders of troops are aware how quickly the wine-shop and the brothel will spoil the soldier. Easy then to conjecture that this life of drinking and idle dissipation was from the first a main cause of the degeneration of the Sword in Germany, and the degradation of the fighting man, who grows ever more and more greedy and mercenary, that he may get the wherewithal to satisfy feminine exactions in the way of ornaments and jewelry.

Notwithstanding the favorable opinion our fathers entertained of these indoor morals, it is open to grave doubt whether the women of the north, eager as they were to rule in the house by playing upon men's sensual appetites, really remained any more chaste and self-restrained in their home life than was their great

---

your thanes, and a great fire kindled in the midmost warms the whole hall, while without all is wrapped in whirling snow . . ."—From the speech of Coïfi, high-priest of the false gods, to Edwy, King of the Northumbrians.—OZANAM, *Les Germains avant le Christianisme*, II.

goddess of love, Freya, in the Olympus of Odin and the northern gods.

The cult of war, the true religion of pagan Scandinavia, which survived to the eleventh century, had from the fifth century downwards descended to a state of the utmost corruption and the lowest ideals; while long before that epoch even, "the goddess Freya played prostitute to all the heavenly heroes and even to mere mortals." Such was the celestial patronage under which domestic life was established and perfected in this purest of all possible worlds, as it has been characterized.

The conclusion to be drawn from the observations thus far brought forward is, that during the epoch of barbarism, the heroic ages of the northern peoples, the Sword conditioned certain distinct and definite virtues among women, whereas on the contrary during civilized periods, these latter have shown a constant tendency to act in such a way as to diminish the strength and dominion of the Sword.

The latter effect, so conspicuous on the farther bank of the Rhine, showed itself in a no less marked degree, but in far more ancient times, south of the Pyrenees and of the Alps,—in these regions contrasting strikingly by the exquisite forms it took with the heavy, dull sensuality of Teutonic lands.

The better to realize this contrast, we should pass at one step from north to south, from the Germany of the Rhine and from Scandinavia, where the wanton, fair-haired Freya dresses her blonde locks with curdled milk, to Iberia, whose lascivious dances are mentioned

by Juvenal and Martial;* then to Italy, where amid
the seductions of intoxicating melody and fragrant perfumes, the brown-locked maids of the South reign as
priestesses of love, myrtle-crowned and amorous.

For the north, we have just seen in what ways
women undertook and carried through the enfeeblement of the Sword.

For the south, we have now to note by what methods
they reduced it to a like state of weakness and decay.

By a close examination of the conditions of ancient
society, some idea may be formed of the authority
women exerted in it by virtue of their charms and
merits under different aspects. Going back to the remote times of the *Iliad*, their amorous activity in war,
so far as the civilization of Southern Europe is concerned, is represented by Helen of Troy and Brisëis.

We find women in those far-off times, to judge by
the accounts of demi-gods and Greek heroes, content
to set the warriors in action without showing any high
degree of emotion themselves. In this way the *non-
chalant* fair ones of those days set the world on fire,
themselves the while curiously consulting the oracles of
shredded rose-leaves. Later again, it was ever with the
same external appearance of inactivity that wantons

---

* "Young wantons of Cadiz (*Gaditanae*) will ply their
loins in lascivious movements, prolonged and artfully seductive."—MARTIAL, *Sat.*

Ad terram tremulo descendant clune puellæ.—JUVENAL,
Sat. "They cower to the ground, shaking their quivering
hips,"—the old Ionian dance.

with painted or veiled face exercised from age to age
their fatal influence over the Sword, whether among
Greeks or Mussulmans.* It is needful thoroughly to
grasp the notion that in Turkey the women, in spite of

---

* "The bride, being of the blood of Othman, has a right to
exact all possible marks of respect from her husband. They
may not see each other openly and freely till after marriage.
The details of the first night of wedded life are regulated
by a strict code of etiquette. In accordance with its laws, a
slave woman must pass the night in the bridal chamber.
The difficult position in which the young man finds himself
may be imagined. His wife is wrapped in veils; after having
lavished on her the formal salutations and exaggerated com-
pliments due to every relative of the Khalif, he humbly begs
her to remove the veils that he may admire without let or
hindrance her radiant beauty.

"Everything depends on this first interview. If the bride-
groom is a man of wit and resource, the fair descendant of
Othman is transformed into a mere woman of mortal flesh
and blood; the slave is turned out of the room, and the
future is assured. Existence will then be endurable for this
consort of a Sultana. . . . Etiquette is exceedingly strict. It
ordains the husband must remain day and night in the part
of the house reserved for the men, the selamlik, at the disposition of his wife. There he must remain in perpetuity.
He only enters the harem on the summons of his wife. He
may not smoke in her presence, nor be absent without her
special authorization."—F. M., in the Temps newspaper.

There is no doubt about the subordinate position held by
the secular husbands of these sacred brides. They may not
enter the marriage bed except by dragging themselves along on
their knees. They must leave it on their bended knees, and
backwards!

"The education of the Mussulman nobility being entrusted
to the women, (the Sultan, Abdul-Hamid, remaining in the
Harem till he was sixteen), this training contributes not a
little to the devirilization of the higher classes."

all appearances to the contrary, have always been just
as powerful as everywhere else. Islam, under its chivalrous European form, represented at our very doors by
the Moors of Spain, who took delight in the intoxication of voluptuous reverie and invented a language of
flowers to express their tenderness in, was invariably,
and more and more as time went on, ruled and influenced by women. The domination of women was a
constant factor with all the ancient peoples of the
south, whose *gladius* (sword), made feminine in *spatha*
and *espada,* offers so sharp a contrast with its fine slenderness and small handle to the massive blades and
enormously elongated hilts of northern weapons.

Be it noted that among such peoples as were true
devotees of lòve, Venus, soul of the universe,* Our
Lady, patroness of chivalry and on occasion pretext for
the duel,† had far more worshippers than any god of
Paganism, or even the Christ himself. In antiquity as
in the Middle Ages, the true religion of soldiers was not
so much Venus,—"not so much the virgin, as *woman.*"

Tenderness towards women, and its corollary respect,
a feeling which warriors of old times instinctively associated with it, existed long anterior to the Christian era
as well in the Roman code of morals as among barbarian peoples, worshippers of the mother of the gods.

---

* Venus, who possessed so many titles significative of her
different qualities, was the first divinity Theseus, king of
Athens, made his people worship.

† Friedrich Heinrich von der Hagen, *Gesammtaben-
teuer,* "A Century of Old German Tales."

The Roman Senate, re-establishing one of the four laws of Romulus,* had decreed that women should, as a mark of public homage, take precedence over men of the Sword,—an equivalent almost for the modern *Lugar a las damas!*—the "Ladies first" of Spanish politeness.

The same principle formed an integral part of the new religious Faith. "The Church," says St. Ambrose, "has it even more nearly at heart to make women respected than to save men from death."

The Visigoths, the Burgundians, the Franks, all professed the profoundest respect for woman as woman; and facts exist to show that the feeling was very general. In Gaul, women possessed for a brief space of time as in Italy, a senate and tribunal deliberating and deciding on the fate of armies. According to the Roman legal code, the man who offended modesty before a patrician dame was liable to be condemned to death, and the *Lex Julia,* no less than the Burgundian laws and those of the Salic Franks, punished with equal severity any insult offered to a free-born woman, or even to a concubine.

The Salic law, by which the maternal line had first right in matters of inheritance,† punished with a fine of 7,500 deniers—an amount, however, soon reduced—

---

* Laws which were engraved on a bronze tablet in the Capitol.

† Women were summoned first to receive inheritances.— J. F. A. PEYRE, *Loi des Franks,* Article under heading LXII.— DAVOUD-OGHLOU, *History of Law among the ancient Germans.* Berlin, 1845.

any one* who had applied the word *harlot* to a free-born maiden, while the ancient code of Salzburg actually assigned the death penalty as the forfeit for rape.

In brief, woman as woman, was in all Europe cherished and respected by the Sword, and protected by its laws. She was the object of a symbolic worship that passed down directly from Pagan idolatry to Christian adoration. Venus, fallen from her high estate, leaves to the Madonna, Saint Mary of the Snows, her world-famous Temple on Mount Eryx.†

Here then we see the man of the Sword at the maximum of his vigor and efficiency, at the point when Lucan admired "his soul that mastered death." Simultaneously we find women in their triumph over brute force at the zenith of their virtues and dominion. This, the highest, culminating point, we must not lose sight of, when later on we come to trace the gradual decrease of virile force and the successive stages of decay in woman's prestige,—in other words, the decay of the feminine ideal.

---

* In our own day in France, the man who insults in the coarsest manner a woman, be she who she may, is liable at law to a fine of from one to sixteen francs. This is removed by a long step from the 7,500 deniers fixed as penalty by the Salic Law! Under Charlemagne the denier was the twelfth part of the silver sou, equivalent to 36 francs of our present money.

† The temple of Venus on Mt. Eryx, once served by a college of courtesan-priestesses, became the Church of Saint Mary of the Snows.—Saint-Augustine, 47, *Publicola.*

A few centuries have sufficed these fair creatures, deified as goddesses by the sons of Mars, to compromise and destroy their own repute. Little by little they have descended voluntarily from their high position, while the warrior has been spoiled by their emasculating influence.

Once they found themselves fortified and embellished, decked out and ennobled, by the Sword, from that moment did they set to work to achieve its absolute subjection. Then later still, by virtue of their clandestine modes of influence and that love of novelty that has ever been at once their stimulus and their ruin, they dragged it down and down through successive stages of degradation,—from the high ideal of chivalry to mere commonplace gallantry, from gallantry to the debaucheries of the most defined sensuality. Such then is the fatal influence of women, an influence represented in fable and legend by Omphalé, by Circé, by the Fairy Morgana.

CHAPTER III

INFLUENCE OF ROYAL MISTRESSES AND CONCUBINES — GIRDLES AND PADLOCKS OF CHASTITY

"No man hath it in his power," Marguerite of Navarre has said in the *Heptameron*, "to over-rule the deceitfulness of a woman." No means of defence are really ours against her and her cajoleries; and yet in every relation uniting her to us, her dishonor involves ours, and her successful wiles expose us to the ridicule of our fellows. This unfair responsibility, still further complicated in former days by questions of pride and mutual jealousy, was at the bottom of all the chief troubles and quarrels of the old fighting, dueling world, that chose to spend its best blood in their adjustment. (So fatally has the all-powerful army of women ever exploited for their own ends the personal valor of the man of the Sword!)

Old traditions affirm that among the barbarians the male child, the *Degenkind* (child of the sword), used to receive its first nourishment after weaning on the point of a sword.* According to other legends the women of Ireland used to pray God their sons might die on the battle-field, while Hungarian mothers were in the habit of biting their boys in the face from their

---

* SOLINUS, ch. XXV.

earliest infancy, wishing by this means to make them more terrifying to the foe. What a contrast these ideas and customs of primitive peoples offer to those of modern times, when mothers are only too strongly tempted to mutilate their male offspring, to render them unfit for military service,—to *spoil* them for the conscription! The same object is attained by their bringing into the world sickly, ill-grown creatures,—a result of their ridiculous tight-lacing.

The enfeeblement of European virility by women's agency may be verified from the Middle Ages downwards, and especially so by looking at the various fashions the swordsman adopted from time to time. His personal vanity is displayed in a disgusting coquetry of costume,—in the shameless (androgynic) forms adopted in his dress or in his accoutrement. Confined at the waist, immoderately expanded at the shoulders, ornamented with enormous artificial organs (cod-pieces), he represents, dressed out in this shameless costume, a sort of two-fold homage paid to the female sex by all that was obscene and effeminate in the male.

For were not all these grotesque absurdities provoked by the one wish to "please the ladies"?

The poets alone, from the earliest dawn of the epic, show us woman disposing, by virtue of love, of the lives and wills of heroes, and turning to her own advantage the enthusiasm of hordes of warriors.

The *Iliad*, the *Edda*, the *Nibelungenlied*, and the romances of chivalry, all establish the fact that the power of love over men's hearts made women the soul of warlike movements. Scandinavian mythology declares how "among the Ases all men lived in peace (in the golden age), till a woman came thither to bring discord and be the cause of the first of all wars."

Greek and Roman no less recognized in their fabulous legends the same principle of discord and disorder, the parent of so many disasters. "The love of women," the poets affirm, "did the Greeks more hurt than ever the arms of the Trojans." Similarly it was Venus who stirred the greatest troubles in Olympus.

There are two distinct categories of women destined in every age to have a decisive bearing upon the doings and exploits of the Sword, and which in a general way must be held responsible for the different phases it undergoes. These are, for the earliest civilized societies of Europe, the patrician dames, matrons or *noble ladies,* in other words, the prolific mothers of the race, owing allegiance to Lucina, and on the other hand the *hetaerae, sphinxes,** unfertile ladies of pleasure, devotees of greed and the wanton Venus—this last class including, though not identical with, the *demi-monde* of Greece and Rome.

These two great castes, mutual rivals, were always brought into intimate contact, at every point along the march of history, by virtue of the striving of mankind after love and beauty, in a word the effort to win plea-

---

* "The hetæræ were called *sphinxes* on account of their unscrupulous rapacity. The sphinx was the emblem of harlots, haunting with their solicitations cross-roads and public squares."

sure. This effort made men raise a golden statue to Phryné, in the days when the Greeks moulded their cups and sacred bowls on the pattern of the bosoms of beautiful courtesans, long before the theatre was defi-nitely consecrated to Venus.*

In this inquiry, it is needless to remark that, in face of the imposing number of noble and distinguished women concerned, the "common clay" of the sex does not come into question at all, peasant-women, house mothers and the like.

The most astounding exploits of knights in the days of chivalry and of swaggering swordsmen and bullies in later times undertaken in honor of fair ladies and mistresses, exploits as a rule marked by an extravagant, not to say ridiculous, character, were all inspired and dictated by the ambitions or merely the unsuccessful combinations and unfulfilled designs of coquettes. As late as the sixteenth century, men often fought simply to win these latter titles, wealth, or at the least some satisfaction to their pride.

After the restrictions imposed on sexual indulgence by the laws of chivalry had fallen into desuetude,

---

* "The theatre was the realm of Venus. When Pompey replaced by stepped seats of marble the wooden platforms on trestles where the old Romans had sat, he dedicated his build-ing to the goddess, whose puissant attraction stirred all Nature."

Three thousand dancing girls, like so many priestesses, served the theatres of Rome; these they kept in the city in time of scarcity, when the Grammarians had to leave the borders.

women of this character proceeded of their own choice
to reward with ample favors any deed of arms that had
advantaged them ever so little. By the adoption of
such a system they once again perverted courage to
unworthy ends. Heroic in its origin, then chivalrous,
presently more and more gross and material, it soon
degenerated into the mere swaggering bravery of gallantry pure and simple. Subsequently we shall see in
detail in what way these successive changes came about.

Francis I of France used to say fair ladies had as
much to do with rendering gentlemen valiant as had
their sword; but we must make no mistake as to the
precise bearing of these flattering words. In these new
deeds of reckless daring, stimulated by foretaste of the
pleasure promised as their reward, there remained nothing whatever of that sentiment of enthusiasm, nothing
of that lofty ideal, which had in preceding ages animated the fray. In their heroic period the barbarian
warriors exposed themselves to death in the "battle-
play" in a single-minded dread of dying of sickness,*
and later again the paladins confronted the most
desperate perils merely to win a smile from some hard-
hearted chatelaine.

The fact is, of what it is the custom nowadays to
call heroism and self-devotion in women of quiet lives
and peaceful dispositions scarcely a single example, of
undoubted sincerity, is offered by earlier ages in con-

---

* Entry into Valhalla was refused to warriors who had
died of disease.—Saxo Grammaticus.—MALLET, Introduction
to the History of Denmark, ch. XIX.

nection with the sword, down to the days when the
Sister of Charity, tenderest incarnation of hope, first
took up her post at the bedside of wounded soldiers.

Our tribute of homage hereby rendered to this the
one solitary and trifling exception to be found (our
investigations stop short of existing social actualities),
it remains to examine the conduct and morality of the
charming and high-placed dames who infatuated the
Europe of our fathers.   All were as thoroughly over-
laid with a traditional suavity and politeness as was
the frail Agnes Sorel,* that "purveyor of naughtiness,"

---

* A judicous chronicler, Georges Chastellain, who lived
in close relations with the court of France in the time of
Agnes Sorel, far from suffering himself to be reduced by the
ascendancy of her beauty and the praises of flatterers, was
struck only by the disrepute into which the king had fallen
and the secret grief and chagrin that consumed the queen.
He enumerates compassionately all the mortal wounds the
heart of the unhappy lady had to endure, when she was
obliged "for peace and quietness' sake," to see her rival
move and have her dwelling day by day along with her;
have her special lodging in the king's house; have company
and rout of women more numerous than her own; see all the
concourse of lords and nobles set towards her; have fairer
bed furniture, better tapestry, better linen and˙clothing, better rings and jewels, better kitchen and better everything.
Yea! all this she had to suffer, and harder still, to take it
cheerfully.

The same writer, a little further on, describes the luxury
Agnes Sorel affected in her toilette, and inveighs against
the improper fashions she set to *modest women.*   "She wore
plaits a third longer than any princess of the kingdom, higher
head-gear, more numerous and more costly dresses.   And of
everything that could make for naughtiness and looseness of
living in the way of dress, of all such she was ever the pur-

that "false prude," as she is described by one of her contemporaries well acquainted with the facts.

My intention in the ensuing inquiry being to proceed solely and entirely on the basis of established facts, I shall invariably refer all objectors to the authenticated documents I have consulted. By dint of a careful examination in their pages of character and conduct, beginning with the holy prophetesses of primitive peoples, and going on to ruling princesses, concubines and mistresses of kings, titled courtesans, veritable queens and princesses of love, representing the fullest scope of women acting with every advantage of position and in the free exercise of their instincts and activites, we shall come to realize the importance and extent of the pernicious effect produced through their appeal to the senses by these fair despots on the worth and well-being of the Sword.

Gaspard de Saulx-Tavannes, a courtier and a soldier, says in his Memoirs written somewhere about 1560: "The domination of women always advances handsome, well-dressed gallants and carpet-knights: 'tis the origin of naughtiness, of ballets, masques, lubricity, ingratitude, cruelty, revenge, discord and unfair dealing; advancing to fortune men and women of shameless lives to the prejudice of stout captains, learned lawyers and men of worth." Such were the unscrupulous ways of these fascinating creatures, these lightheaded, false-

veyor and ensample, for that she displayed her shoulders and bosom in front down to the middle of the breast." QUICHERAT, *Histoire du Costume.*

hearted beings, who in their sovereign recklessness make their own caprice the sole criterion of good and evil, and exalt love above virtue. They have invariably turned to evil ends the heroism of lovers, the tender gallantry of warriors, of knights, crusaders and of gentlemen, and the diplomacy of the delegates of the Sword. Instances exist to show how in all periods the balance of right and justice has been biased; while petty frivolities are allowed to become the causes of duels or of war. The Italian War, Brantôme declares, was decided on by Francis I of France for no other reason except that he might at Milan see and enjoy the charms of the fascinating Signora Clerice.* There is no doubt that the beauty of the courtesans of Lombardy disastrously prolonged the French occupation of that country, and was partly responsible for its failure. Finally, as a last example of the same dangerous influence, Buckingham, cajoled by the coquetries and favors of Anne of Austria, armed England against France in 1527.

A weapon of weight at the court of princes, the sword, it was said, "was an inborn prerogative of nobility." They owed everything to it; and every excess was forgiven it, crime and betrayal in love, assault and assassination. Women, always indulgent

---

* Admiral de Bonnivet had spoken to King Francis I, of the "*Signora* Clerice," and "had made the king long to see her and sleep with her: and so this was the principal reason for that expedition—a reason few suspect. For indeed, one half of the world does not know how the other half lives, etc." —BRANTOME, *Grands Capitaines* (Admiral de Bonnivet).

critics of the vices themselves inspire, always touched
by a crime committed to please them, paid liberally
with their persons for such trifling services as this.
About the year 1554 the sword saved the Parisian ladies
from the hateful introduction of the invidious chastity-
belts of Bergamo, an imitation of the ancient Roman
padlocked guards.*

---

* The chastity-belt, or safety belt, of the Italians and
Spaniards, is intended. "Bergamo is a town of Italy where
they sell and make use of many of these belts."—LE DUCHAT,
Notes sur Rabelais.

"Unless I plug my wife, as do the Bergamasques."—Rabelais, Pantagruel, bk. III, ch. XXXVI.

"This precaution, which sundry Italians have deemed
good to take with their wives, was what some thought of intro-
ducing into France in the sixteenth century." Brantôme
relates the fact in his Dames Galantes.

"In the days of King Henri," he says, "there was a certain jeweler who imported at the fair of St. Germain a
dozen of certain contrivances to bridle women's affairs.
These were constructed of iron, and encircled the waist
like a girdle or belt; they passed underneath, and could be
secured there with a lock,—being so cunningly framed that
the woman, once bridled therewith, could never avail for
the pleasures of love, as the things were pierced but by
a few minute holes. . . .

"Many gentlemen of the court could not endure to see
the commerce the Italian merchant had of these padlocked
guards; and threatening to throw him in the river if he continued the said traffic, they constrained the man to give up
the trade. Since that day no one has dreamed in France of
having these guards made, or of having them brought out of
Italy."

Nevertheless, in spite of Brantôme's statement of opinion
a "brayer de fer" (iron truss) or chastity-belt is mentioned
in the Historiettes, No. 473, related by Tallemant des Réaux.

See also *Playdoyer contre l'introduction des cadenas ou ceintures de chasteté* (Plea as against the Introduction of "Guards" or Chastity-belts), by FREYDIER, Montpelier, 1750, 8vo, with a plate representing the contrivance in question.

(A *chastity-belt* is to be seen in excellent preservation among the treasures of the Musée Cluny in Paris; and no less than three of them were exhibited in London in 1892 in the very curious and valuable collection of instruments of torture made by the Duke of Buckingham and Chandos, which also contained the famous "Iron Maiden" of Nüremberg. All three *cadenas* were delicately made of thin hoop iron, padded where necessary, and still covered with the remains of figured silk or satin.)—Translator.

CHAPTER IV

SWORDSMEN BECOME THE AGENTS OF WOMEN'S
SEXUAL EXCESSES — PUBLIC DEFIANCES
CONCERNING HARLOTS

At the very first glance it is found that, dating from
the best days of chivalry onwards, with all that was
most distinguished among dashing, dainty dames, the
Sword had undisputed command of all advantages.
Always fond and festive, always at lovemaking in times
of leisure, always showing a gallant affectation of
reckless gaiety and ease of manner, it represented in
the eyes of women yet other telling and seductive
qualities. It was an indispensable ally in their indulgences, giving a certain flavor of "high life" to their
caprices, a surfeit of caresses after battles fought and
victories won, presents from overseas and fresh news
of the great outside world. It guaranteed the most
sensual and irresponsible impunity in fast living, precedence over a hated rival, romance in adultery or
intrigue, nay! even in detection and scandal, assassination effectually killing ridicule,—a thing always more
shameful from the feminine point of view than dishonor. It could give them nobility,* in other words,

* "Women had not the right to be entitled *ladies* (*dames*)
until their husbands had been made knights. Before that

the right to be proud and prettily dressed, could make them rich after a campaign and famous after a tournament—for "a lover slain for their sake brought them great repute." Then again, a principle outweighing all the rest put together, the Sword, that thwarted and annihilated all sumptuary laws, was the most convincing preacher and advocate of luxurious living and pleasure. Humble servant of ladies' wishes, it afforded them instant protection against offences of every kind, the laws being far too slow in operation to please their childish caprice, always fain to reverse the hourglass before the hour is run.

It was the special duty and privilege of the Sword to be the agent of women's politics, of their everlasting love of intrigue and not seldom of their personal vengeance, offering them the chance, better than did sorcery or witchcraft, of freedom in a sudden and premature widowhood that was always among its possibilities. St. Jerome relates how in the early days of the legalization of divorce a certain matron had seventeen husbands in less than a year.* Last but not least, the Sword could silence "forked tongues, indiscreet,

---

they were called merely *damoiselles*."—LA CURNE DE SAINTEPALAYE, *Memoires sur l'Ancienne Chevalerie*.

* SAINT JEROME, *Epist. XCI, ad Ageruchiam, de Monogamia*.

"In less than thirty days," Martial (V. 1. 7.) tells us, "Thelesilla is already at her tenth husband. So many marriages are nothing but legalized adulteries."

In Tacitus' day, the Roman ladies were forever changing their husbands.

envious and ill-conditioned mouths," no less than timid or easy-natured husbands, who made no scruple of taking advantage of its forbidden fruits.

Thus, thanks to the Sword, "small wonder, then, if the Lady Polygamy doth prance and kick, doth play the wanton and corrupt all with her adulterous excesses!" Relying on the impunity his protection gave her, the mistress of a ruffler, a *Gladiator*—by this name was still known as late as 1640, the duelist, the stickler for the point of honor—would show off, "nosegay at ear,"* sundry little airs of studied arrogance, sundry little ways and tricks of toilette, alluring or triumphant, specially affected by the favorites of the rapier. "To walk abroad protected by her *shadow*,† and on that account to be feared and respected by all women and all men"—did not this constitute a supreme form of gratification for a woman's vanity?

So in the world of dress and flirtation, where this particular infatuation raged like an epidemic, the great question was who should have as *cavaliere servante*

---

* "Le bouquet sur l'oreille," a phrase alluding to the old French country custom of attaching a nosegay to beasts for sale. So people say in jest: "Cette fille a le bouquet sur l'oreille," such and such a girl is on the market, is on the lookout. (Translator.)

† "The Spanish women love to walk proudly, protected by the shadow of some Captain, whom they keep with money they earn from rich lovers."

Y ser a su sombre respetada y tormida de tos y de todos; i. e., "to be by one's shadow respected and feared of all women and all men."—QUEVEDO, *Obras escogidas* (Select Works).

the keenest blade, *delle più forbite* (one of the most
highly polished), that is to say, the most brilliant champion, though perhaps not always the most lavish in
presents, one "having the look of a desperado that
knew well how to chastise fools to teach them to speak
discreetly of ladies."*

Cobarruvias in his Dictionary has described and
defined a gallant of the sort. "The *espadassin,*" he
says, "is a champion who walks abroad with a swagger,
his hand on the pommel of his sword, keeping its point
tilted in the air."

Does not this peep at *a Spanish ruffler* in the act
help us to guess at all the successes and favors with
the ladies such a bearing and attitude must needs have
won?

To these various causes of success with women
might easily be added a number of others. Ever since
classical times, when the Sword as a career was ranked
by Xenophon above any other profession, when a
simple courtesan was foundress of the Floralia or Floral
Games,† or offered to rebuild at her own charge towns

---

* BRANTOME, Opuscule XVI, p. 492.

† The Floral Games, founded by the courtesan Flora, were
restored again by the fair Isaurian.

This account of the foundation of the Floralia rests solely
on the authority of Lactantius (*Institut.* 1.20). The indecency
that accompanied their celebration is probably the only ground
for the story. As a matter of fact the Floralia were appar-
ently instituted at Rome in 238 B.C., on the occasion of the
dedication of a temple to the goddess Flora by the Aediles,
L. and M. Publicius, in the Circus Maximus at the command
of an oracle in the Sibylline books, for the purpose of ob-

destroyed in war, the devotees of him of the Golden
Sword—every woman, high or low, loves to receive
presents—have lived on victorious soldiers; except,
of course—but this is of comparatively rare occurrence
—when pleasure carried the day against self-interest,
and the parts were reversed, the gallant living at the
charges of his *inamorata*. In France this reversed order
of things is found embodied in an old custom. By
virtue of a certain feudal privilege, damsels of gay and
independent habits, in other words "of irrepressible
conduct and merry life," were in some cases farmed
and taxed by the Sword; while in Italy courtesans paid
as highly as they could afford their champions or *bravi*
—the name given to the swordsmen whose office it
was to defend and keep them in countenance.*

Among all the high qualities of the Sword there
existed one more desirable than all others to raise its
prestige in the minds of women. This was the power
which the champions of love had of publicly consecrat-
ing the beauty of such or such a fickle fair one by
proclaiming her handsomer than her rivals.

The defiance addressed to Monsieur de Villars by

---

taining the divine protection for the yearly blossom (ut
omnia bene deflorescent).—PLINY, *Nat. Hist.* XVIII, 286.
Similar, but informal, festivals first in the country and afterwards introduced into towns, had long been common in all
parts of Italy in the Spring. (Translator)

* BRANTOME, *Grands Capitaines*, (Henri II).

"Like the courtesans of Italy and Rome, who will always
have a *bravo*, for thus they call him, to defend and keep them
in countenance."—BRANTOME, *Dames Galantes.*

the Earl of Essex, lover of Queen Elizabeth*—Queens' favorites are invariably men of the sword—concluded with these words, calling to mind the old-world phrases of French chivalry which still to some extent survived at the court of England: "I am a better man than you, and my mistress is fairer than yours." Surrey, being at Florence, had a challenge or *cartel* of the same sort placarded on the walls there, addressed to "all Christians, Jews, Moors, Turks and Cannibals," in which he, Surrey, as against all and sundry, maintained the incomparable beauty of Geraldine.

Nor were these flattering manifestos on the part of the gallants displayed solely in favor of ladies "of high degree," or well-born *demoiselles*. The *fair ladies of mirth and merriment*, the *hirondelles de clocher* (steeple swallows), as they are entitled by a law of 1521, likewise found bold blades to proclaim the superiority of their charms. This was particularly the case in Italy, where the women, like those of Spain, were always partial to rufflers, knifers with their scarred faces, and even brigands.

In the work of Fausto da Longiano† are to be found

---

* L'Estoile, *Journal du règne de Henri IV,* vol. I, p. 144, notes. The edition of 1741, printed at the Hague.

† No ruffler or *bravo* was reputed valorous and a man of honor that had not ill-reputed and immodest women in the places of evil reputation, kept there for public traffic, thus acquiring the title of *palese ruffiano* (accredited ruffian, or bully).

These *ruffiani* had adopted the custom of challenging by *cartels* or public defiances, some of these being drawn up in

the terms of sundry cartels such as the wandering *bravi*
used to nail up on the doors of their favorites to

---

the name of the whole *scola* (college) of the *bravos* of Bologna
or of Naples. As an instance of the terms employed in such
defiances, here is one,—a cartel of a *bravo* of Milan to one
of Rome:

"You may have heard tell how I have always made profession of having fair harlots (*putte*), and how many of such
I have at the instant in ward (*balia*). I have been informed
lately there is come to you such a one by name Perina,
exceeding handsome. So, unless you will of your free will
send the same to me, or transmit me word that I may send
to take her to go along with mine, hold yourself in readiness
to make good your refusal, etc."

The following is the answer of the Roman to the Milanese:

"You are not the sort of fellow that a man of my sort
need take account of your profession. Perina belongs to me,
and is perfectly handsome. You shall bring as against her
two of your women, of a surety less handsome and less
worthy, who shall be at my disposal if I win the day, to be
Perina's servants in all ways that shall seem good to her.
And indeed, even were she less handsome, less amiable and
less gentle, none the less would I maintain her to surpass
yours in beauty and amiability and up-bringing."

These *bravi* errant sometimes issued a *general cartel* to the
following effect for all the towns where they arrived with
their *putte*:

Cartel of a *bravo* errant as regarding his *female companions*:

"Whatsoever man of honor there be that shall dare affirm
that the *women* (*femine*, light women) whom I bring hither
in my company are not the handsomest, most amiable and
most gentle of all such as dwell in this city, I hereby offer to
fight with him in public or in private lists with no matter
which of the weapons our like make use of."—FAUSTO DA
LONGIANO, *Duello del tempo cavalieri errante, de bravi, et de
leta nostra.* . . .

vaunt their charms. At the chamber-door of the
cantoneras, the light o' loves, of Old Castile, each
client used to hang up in sign of protection to his
chosen fair one his rapier and dagger before going in.*
Not difficult to guess the many advantages which the
noble courtesans—for under this title were known the
most superior of the ladies of pleasure at Rome in the
century during which the fair Imperia† flourished—
reaped from their associations with the Sword. For
ladies have in all ages, from the times of the Roman
matrons, whose peace of mind was disturbed by the
gains and triumphs of the courtesans of the flowered
robes,‡ taken toll of victorious soldiers in the form of

* On going in to *ladies of pleasure,* it was customary in
Spain (about 1660) to "leave at the door of their chamber
sword and dagger, and so any that came there afterward,
seeing these weapons hung up there, withdrew without further
word."—ARSENS DE SOMMERDYCK, *Journey in Spain,* 1665.

† One of the first to be known under the name of *noble
courtesans* was the fair Imperia, on whose tomb in the Church
of Saint Gregorio on the Celian was engraved the following
epitaph:

*Imperia, cortisana romana, quae, digna tanto nomine, rarae
inter homines formae specimen dedit; vixit annos XXVI, dies
XII; obiit 1511, die 15 Augusti.* (Imperia, a Roman courtesan, who, well worthy to bear so high a name, gave an example amongst men of most rare beauty; she lived twenty-six
years and twelve days; and died in the year 1511, on August
15.)

In her day, a medal was struck in her honor. Bandello
and Negri spoke of her in their writings as a *noble courtesan
of Rome.* "Imperia, a noble courtesan at Rome, as you are
aware," wrote Negro, in 1532, to Marc-Antony Micheli.

‡ *Courtesans of the flowered robes,* that is to say, wearing

presents, and won fine clothes out of their lovers'
martial generosity.*

From Perseus to the Marquis de Létorrières,† very
few fighting legends exist in which is not to be found

---

in accordance with a decree of the Areopagus, flowered robes,
variegated and embroidered in different hues, intended to
distinguish them from the matrons and virgins, clad in public
in more simple attire.—SUIDAS, *Lexicon*.

* "To deck her fairly withal before God and all men," a
knight offered his lady a complete outfit.—OLIVIER DE LA
MARCHE, *Le Parement et triomphe des dames* (The Bedizen-
ing and Triumph of Fair Ladies), of the fifteenth century.
In the romance of *Berte aux grands pieds* (thirteenth century), we see how such as brought them presents were welcomed by wives or mistresses.

† Louis XV died, and Létorrières, well known as having
attended the king in his sickness, made haste to go and fight
with the champion of Savoy, who gave him two wounds in
a single lunge in the right side. M. de Létorrières was put
to bed and his wounds treated; his door was kept shut, and
the news given out that he had caught the king's disease.
His wounds were most severe; but this did not prevent him
after two more days of treatment, from being off to scale the
walls of the Abbey of Montmartre, and once inside to spend
the night by the side of Mlle. de Soissons, under the great
vaulted arcade that leads from the cloisters to the Cemetery.
. . . It appears the Princess prudently returned home before
day-break, and the unhappy girl never saw her gallant lover
again. The latter's wounds had reopened; his blood escaped
to the last drop during the night, as no doubt he preferred not
to call for any help. Next morning he was found stretched
stone dead on the flags of the Cloister. The dreadful business was hushed up. . . . The body was superb; M. de
Létorrières was carried back to his bed, and was announced
to have died of the smallpox."—*Souvenirs de la marquise de
Créquy.*

figuring, now mixed up with magic and marvels, now with the dramas of history, some woman, the instrument of doom by her love or her greed.

In the martial politics of the Olympus of Greece and Rome, in the warlike mythology of the Scandinavians, in the traditions of pagan Iceland, in the Christian myths, where a captive lady represents Religion delivered by the Sword, in the romances of the Middle Ages, in the emblems of chivalry, everywhere, as well in fact as in fiction, are to be found conjoined these two ideas, these two words, sword and sex, love and war, symbolized by Freya in the arms of Odin, the slave of the magic necklace* and by Venus wantoning with Mars, even in the guise of planets.†

Look into old Chronicles, listen to the gossip of ancient tales and *Nouvelles,* and you will find how the Sword, everywhere and always, took art and part in quarrel for some cherished fair one.   The duel was

---

* Freya did what she pleased with Odin by dint of the necklace (*brinsgamen*) which the dwarfs forged for her.— This magic necklace reminds us of the girdle of Venus, the charm of which mastered the gods. "It was wrought with the needle and colored in variegated hues; it had in it all pleasures, love, longing, amorous converse and gentle words." Juno borrowed it of Venus, to make herself loved.

† "There is no planet loved of Mars but Venus only,—as the Astrologers do hold."—SCIPION DUPLEY, Paris, 1602, ch. VIII, p. 45.

In the Mineralogical science of the seventeenth century, the *Vitriolum Veneris* represents Venus; under this form, she takes such strong hold of Mars, that is iron, when she is in contact with it "that at the last she doth substitute her own proper body and maketh that of Mars to disappear."

in its origin based on love.* Even the favorites, the
mignons of the emasculated Valois fight and kill one
another, " and that for ladies' sake," Brantôme declares.†

Wherever men fought, it was for their honor and to
defend their honor. The swordsman carried "the
honor—forfeit or no, it made no matter—of his lady
on his sword's point, so that no man durst assail it."‡
Then he goes on—it is still Brantôme speaking—
naïvely betraying the ideas of his time on such subjects, to add bluntly: "Is it then after all so great a
crime for a woman in return for such services to give
some little courteous favor of her body?"§ Not a
few, indeed, of the "gentle and honorable ladies" of the
time were fain to grant such recompense. The Sword,
master of every art of allurement, offered a standing
excuse for women's caprice, while men's daring intre-
pidity induced women to lightly regard the importance
of the merely physical.

It fell out once, an old Italian legend relates, that a
virtuous lady of great beauty, by name Desdemona,

---

* "We have seen, and still see every day, so many examples
to prove that fights for love occur no less frequently than
for honor."—SCIPION DUPLEY, *Les lois militaires touchant
le duel.* Paris, 1602; ch. VIII, p. 45, Of Duels Originating
in Love.

† "I will begin my relation with Quielus and Antraguet,
noted fighters, and that for ladies."—BRANTOME, *Discours
sur les duels.*

‡ BRANTOME, *Dames galantes.*

§ BRANTOME, *Discours sur les duels,* edition by Buchon.

"grew love-sick for a Moor,"*—who, so the tradition
says, was a man of a most admirable courage. Three
hundred years later, about 1780, the Chevalier de
Saint-Georges the finest swordsman of his day, enjoyed
the favors of all the greatest ladies of Versailles, though
he was of the same complexion as Othello. "The brave
have no need of beauty."

Such was the universal opinion during the warlike
ages—that gallant ladies admire and prefer daunt-
less men. Queen Isabella of Castile was wont to say
she knew no sight in all the world so fine as a fighting man in the field, unless it were a beautiful woman
in her bed.

The classical texts reveal the fact that feminine infatuation for the Sword had at the date of the Caesars
reached the height of its paroxysm. "His eyes were
blood-shot, his countenance coarse and ignoble, but
then he was a Gladiator! That name makes them as
beautiful as Hyacinthus . . . *Ferrum est quod amant!*
—'Tis the sword they love," exclaims Juvenal,† indig-
nant at seeing wives of senators, patrician ladies, in
love like the Empress Faustina‡ with common fencers,

---

* GIO BATTISTA GIRALDI CINTIO, *De gli Ecatommiti*, seventh
nouvelle of the third decade, in the French translation of
Gabriel Chapuys. The use Shakespeare has made of the story
in "Othello" is too familiar to need more than mention.

† "He was ignoble, *but* he was a Gladiator; by virtue
of this name Hippia sets him before her children, her country, her sisters and her husband. . . . 'Tis the sword they
love!"—JUVENAL, *Sat. VI.*

‡ Being at Gaëta, Faustina, who had married Marc Antony,

and fighting all stripped in the Roman circuses. It is indeed the *ferrum* (iron), the sword, that seduces them; for once mistresses of it, the noble weapon *par excellence*, which from Arria's time marks the highest tragic note they are capable of, they grow emboldened and claim men's rights. They add to the passive courage they have always displayed as mothers or as martyrs, an odd, freakish spirit of reckless daring, and henceforth feel equal to all and every audacity,— though there always remains discernible a touch of the temper of the hero who died of fright at the notion of the end of the world's coming.

The laws of the Ripurian Franks* recognized,

---

gave herself up body and soul to the gladiators; she composed, to celebrate the death of one of their number, according to what Polyphilus says, a certain lengthy epitaph.

"Others again are infatuated with a Gladiator."— PETRONIUS, *Satyricon*.

Among the female gladiators who fought all stripped in the Circus were wives of senators and ladies of the highest rank.—TACITUS, *Annals*, XV.

"At that period was held a combat of women. Although they fought bravely, having been chosen with this end among noble ladies at a special meeting, . . ."—DIO CASSIUS, *Hist. Rom.*, bk. XXXVI.

Victoria, mother of Victorinus and imperial ruler of Gaul, married for love Marius, a sword-maker.

* According to the laws of the Franks, in certain cases of separation claimed by a woman dissatisfied with her husband, the former was presented with a distaff (*conucula*) and a sword. If she chose the sword, she became free again, but on the condition of killing the husband, who represented servitude for her.

under certain conditions of separation, the wife as possessing a right to make a choice between a distaff and
a sword. If she repented her complaint, she chose the
distaff, emblem of servitude and submission, and must
say to her husband, "My gentle lord, your humble servant!"* a traditional formula in use throughout the
Middle Ages. On the contrary if, formally and before
the judges, she seized the sword, she became free
again at law, on the condition of killing her husband—
the very issue of which in a later century and without
sanction of law, Francesca Bentivoglio† and Mlle. de
Châteauneuf‡ brought things to!

Yet another point serving to explain the favor
accorded by women to the sword, the special weapon
of gentlemen—it must be remembered how in all ages
it has played a part as one of the properties of nocturnal gallantries. Formerly the king of Spain never

---

The distaff was, from ancient times onwards, the symbol
of submission on the part of the wife.

* "My lord, behold me your humble servant." Thus spoke
she who held by the distaff, having accepted the *sou* and
denier.—Formules de Marculphe, bk. II, ch. XXVII.

† "Francesca Bentivoglio, seeing her husband make a successful stand against the four assassins she had concealed
under the bed to kill him, herself sprang from her bed and
seized a sword, with which she struck him down."—VALERY,
Voyages en Italie, vol. II, bk. VII, ch. I.

‡ "The *demoiselle* de Châteauneuf, one of the king's favorites before he went into Poland, having made a love
match with Antinotti, a Florentine, commander of the galleys
at Marseilles, and having caught him playing the rake, slew
him gallantly with her own hand." L'ESTOILE, *Journal,*
Sept., 1577.

went to the queen's chamber without his long espada
(sword) under his arm,* and fortunate gallants never
failed, once in their mistress's room, to hang their
sword, in case of surprise, at the bed's head. It was,
for lovers, the trusty guard that would feel no scruples
in ridding them of a jealous husband or unsuccessful
rival. "All is fair at night," Philippe de Commines
said. The honored weapon which the Castilians used
to kiss every morning like a holy relic† dignified even
murder, and was sometimes said "to be a fairy-sword."‡

Moreover, the fact must never be lost sight of that,
as a means of providing summary justice then and
there, it established a certain equilibrium in married
life, a certain mutual respect between man and wife
—those two individuals always inimical, yet bound
together in fetters of love. Thus not a few gallant
dames, from heroic times down, have taken delight, as
did the Canaanitish women of old.§ Women indeed

---

* "The king still has his great sword in one hand and the
dark lantern in the other. He is bound to go thus accoutred
all alone into the queen's chamber."—Mme. d'Aulnoy,
Relation du Voyage d'Espagne (Account of my Spanish Journey), vol. III.

† Mme. d'Aulnoy, Relation du Voyage d'Espagne, 1879;
The Hague, 1705, vol. III.

‡ "A sword with a handle of iron and cross-hilted, known
as the sword of Lancelot of the Lake; and 'tis said it is a
fairy-sword."—Inventory of the ancient Arms preserved at
the Castle of Amboise, of the time of Louis XII. (Sept.,
1499).

§ "Cardinal de Cusa deems that this prohibition for a
man to wear women's clothes, and for a woman to wear

are nothing if not gluttons of public notice, hence
witches—twenty instances of these for every two of
wizards;* hence again female demoniacs, who took a
positive pride in their possession by the foul fiend.

A word or two as to their primitive arms. At first
it was slave-women who in honor of a dead master of
wealth and magnificence slew each other at his tomb;
later, the exaltation taking on a new character but
still manifesting itself in paroxysms of contagious enthusiasm, grew after centuries of toleration, or better say at once, encouragement, into a form of madness.

The female gladiators of Rome, having brought
discredit on the patrician matrons in the Circus, led to
combats being forbidden in which women fought in
companies with each other, or women with dwarfs,†
such combats being no less reprobated by Christianity.
Swordswomen do not appear any more at all conspicuously till towards the end of the Middle Ages, and

---

those of a man, has reference to idolatry; for that the Canaanitish women used to wear the accoutrements and arms of
men, in honor of Mars, while the men dressed themselves as
women, for Venus' sake."—PHILIPPE CAMERARIUS, *Médi-
tations historiques*, vol. II, part II, ch. XIX.

* The German Monk, Sprenger, in his manual of the
Inquisition, or "Witches' Hammer," asks the question why
there are so few wizards and so many witches, and why the
Devil has such a better understanding with women.
Later on he endeavors to explain this by noting the natural
tendency of women towards all sorts of emotional excesses.

† DIO CASSIUS, *Hist. Rom.*, bk. LXXVI, mentions a combat of women, among whom figured as female gladiators
ladies of the Roman patriciate.

then only in isolated cases as heroines or adventuresses. From that time forth they are divided into two quite distinct categories, viz., mystics or heaven-inspired enthusiasts on the one part, and giddy-pated swaggerers on the other, the two several classes being represented in France by the visionary Jeanne d'Arc and, at a much later date, by the actress Mlle. de Maupin, no less famous in fencing than expert in naughtiness.*

---

* The most famous of all petticoated duelists was the actress Maupin, of whom exploits in this kind of a truly astonishing nature are told. She was born in Paris in 1673, her father being named Daubigny. She married young, and after sending her husband away into the provinces with a post in the taxes, entered the Opera in 1698 as an actress. Passionately fond of fencing, she entered into a liaison with Serane, a fencing-master, and gained such a mastery over her weapon as almost eclipses that attained at a later day by the Chevalier, or Chevalière, d'Eon. Being one day insulted by the actor Dumény, her colleague, she lay in wait for him in the Place des Victoires, and having failed to induce him to take sword in hand, carried off his watch and snuff-box. Another of her colleagues having similarly insulted her, she compelled him to ask her pardon on his knees.

"La Maupin was a Sappho, if not in wit, at any rate in habits, and she had the effrontery to be proud of it. Being present once at a ball, she allowed herself certain indecent and provocative gestures toward a lady. Three gentlemen who accompanied the latter tried in vain to stop her. She challenged them, forced them to leave the room with her and killed all three. After this little interlude, she returned quite quietly into the ball-room again." She was pardoned by the king eventually, her biographer says.

She retired to Brussels, where she became the mistress of the Elector of Bavaria.

CHAPTER V

WARLIKE CAPRICES OF THE FAIR SEX — "MERRY MAIDENS" OR LADIES OF THE CAMP

Following the instinct of imitation attributed to sheep by Panurge, the feminine spirit of combativeness, which is nothing else at bottom but a blustering kind of coquetry, spread far and wide in Europe from the fifteenth century onwards. From that date on, it pro-duced among the fantastic sex many strange tricks in mimicry of the hectoring ways of men.

Observe this: southern lands have always produced these women of the sword in far greater numbers than temperate or cold climes. Apart from the amazons of Bohemian legend, the shield maidens* of Iceland, and a few Teutonic female champions, very few warlike women are heard of, since barbarian times, in the North of Europe. On the other hand in Italy, the land where Luca de Pulci† and Ariosto dreamed of their far-famed warrior-maids, there were several different types of *cavalieressi* (lady-cavaliers). This name, so

---

* The shield-maidens.—H. WHEATON, *History of the Northmen or Danes and Normans*. This is an American work, first published in 1831. There is a French translation by Guillot, Paris (Marc-Aurèle) 1844.

† Luca de Pulci, *Ciriffo Calvaneo*, p. 25 of Florence edi-tion, 1834.

suggestive of charm and airy grace, was equally applicable to the "very noble Luzia Stanga," to the famous
Margheritona,* who served as a trooper in a company
of light-horse, or lastly to the courtesan Malatesta,
mentioned by Bandello, who used to go forth at night
to her love adventures armed with a *rotella* (small
round shield) and a sword.† Religious recluses,

* "A girl named Margheritona, a courtesan, served for pay
as a trooper in the squadron of light horse of the Count de
Gaiazzo."—BANDELLO, *Fifteenth Novella*, dedication.

Bandello likewise mentions as *cavalieressi* or swordswomen
"the very noble Luzia Stanga, who, sword in hand, intimi-
dates many brave men"; also the daughter of the gardener
of the very learned Signor Alessandro Bentivoglio, who defended her father, the latter being unarmed, against two
sbirri (police agents). Having put hand to sword, she killed
one of the constables and gave the other a sword thrust.
Lastly, he speaks of a beautiful Greek girl named Marcella,
who, at the siege of Counio by the Turks, on seeing her
father slain at her feet, seized his sword and *rotella*, and
driving back the Turks, killed several of them, and finally
drove them out of the island.

† Bandello, created Bishop of Agen by Henri II in 1550,
relates in his 50th Novella, that in his time (1504-1515)
there dwelt at Lyons a certain courtesan of the name of
Malatesta, who was accustomed to go at night-time to her
assignations armed with a sword and *rotella*, which she
knew how to use in a very bold and very dexterous fashion.
"Ella di notte con la sua spada a la rotella partiva dall
albergo." (She a-nights with her sword and her *rotella*,
would forth from the inn.)

Henri Beyle states that Bandello invented nothing in his
Novelle, and says all of them are founded on actual occur-
rences.—STENDHAL, *Promenade dans Rome* (A Walk in
Rome).

moreover, beyond the Alps, at times donned the sword, when they went disguised as gallants to assignations to enjoy the gaieties of the carnival.*

Spain, where at the present day enterprising young women are to be seen taking the part of *espadas* at the bull-fights at which young bulls are baited, had, no less than Italy, its fighting women in the days when its *manolas* (common wenches) wore the *cuchillo*

---

* "Moreover, on those days it is not forbidden the recluses to dress up as gentlemen, with velvet caps on their heads, tight fitting hose, and having sword at side."—LE LASCA, *Introduzione al Novellare* (Introduction to the Art of Novel-writing).

"As late as the eighteenth century, nuns in Italy carried the stiletto. An Abbess thus armed fought with another lady for the Abbey of Pomponne."—LE PRESIDENT DE BROSSES, *Lettres familières écrites d'Italie.* (Familiar Letters from Italy), vol. I.

Such licence was at its height towards the end of the seven-teenth century. An example is afforded by "the reckless folly of Madame de Fontenac, a religious recluse at Poissy, who, not content with playing the harlot generally, set her mind upon dancing a ballet with five other nuns and their six gallants. They went to St. Germain, where the king was at the time. It was supposed at first the ballet had come out from Paris; but by next morning the real truth was known."—TALLEMANT DES REAUX, Note to the *Historiette No.* 69, Cardinal de Richelieu.

"Nuns indulge in riotous living, receiving masks handed them through the convent *grilles.* Also they disguise them-selves in all sorts of ways. They go to the play, and you can feast with them at tables made on purpose, the one half of which is inside, the other half outside, the *grille* of the parlors in their convents."—MISSON, *Voyage d'Italie,* 1668, vol. II.

(poniard)* in their garters, which were embroidered with various mottos.

Cervantes in one of his Romances relates as quite an ordinary incident of his day, how a young man practices arms with his mistress, a *muy diestra* (most skilful hand).† Another skilful lady-fencer again is mentioned in the *Diable Boiteux;* and a very curious Chronicle records the fact that a certain nun of Spanish origin, Doña Catalina de Erauso,‡ known as the *monja alferez* (the nun-ensign), who longed to be a Captain like the "Virgin del Pilar" (Virgin of the Pillar)§ in the Aragonese ballad, was famous in the

---

* *Las del cuchillo en la liga,* "they of the poniard in their garter." This was the name given in old Spanish to the *manolas* thus armed. Their garters were embroidered with gallant mottos of this sort: "I shall be beautiful as the rose."—"You are soft as honey."—"Lovely as Rachel."—"The fine lady prefers lilac garters."—"Love gives happiness, especially in solitude."—BARON DAVILLIER, *Voyage d'Espagne.*

† LUIS VELEZ DE GUEVARA, *El Diabolo cojuelo.* ("Le Diable Boiteux," The Limping Devil.)

‡ "The ruffler Doña Catalina de Erauso, nicknamed the *Monja Alferez,* that is, the nun-ensign, fought a large number of duels between the years 1607 and 1645, killing several of her opponents and getting severely wounded herself in some of these encounters.

"Dressed in men's clothes after the Spanish mode, she professes herself a swordsman, and carries her sword with spirit."—PEDRO DEL VALLE.

§ The Virgin del Pilar, in accordance with a curious Portuguese custom which gave the saints in vogue such a rank in the army, was in 1808 nominated by the Aragonese Captain-General of their troops, as a *Jota* (Catch) of the time has it:

years 1607 to 1645 for the fights and duels she engaged in.

In the northern regions of Europe hardly a single instance is to be found of a genuine martial heroine, with the one exception of Hannah Snell, an English-woman, nicknamed the "girl-soldier."* She was a late

---

La Virgen del Pilar dice
Que no quiere ser Francese,
Que quiere ser capitana
De la tropa aragonesa.

"The Virgin del Pilar says she will not be a Frenchwoman, that she will be Captain of the army of Aragon."

On the day of his coronation, the king of Spain, after the *Te Deum*, makes his way to the chapel in which stands the statue of the Virgen del Pilar, an image more highly revered than God himself by all Aragon. It is a small figure of wood, dressed up in precious stuffs so as to leave only the head of the Virgin visible, surrounded by a dazzling aureole. It is a privilege accorded to the king only, to kiss this Virgin.

In the last century, many towns and provinces in Spain still had each their own special Virgin.

* Hannah Snell was born at Worcester in 1723. She served with credit in the army and died pensioned by her country.

Another Englishwoman, who lived to 108, may also be mentioned as having worn the sword in service. In her youth she had enlisted in the 5th regiment of foot. At the battle of Fontenoy she was wounded in the arm by a bayonet thrust. George IV granted her a pension of 10 shillings a week.

These two instances of soldierly heroines, however, really have, except incidentally, nothing to do with our subject. England, like the northern countries generally, has never produced any swordswomen strictly so called. I am sure of this, owing to the kind and able help of Mr. George Chapman, who has been so good as to carry out at my suggestion

survival and representative in that country of the
stalwart swordswomen who in other lands wore the
rapier and made a noise in the world of an earlier
day. In France, on the contrary, their exploits were
frequent enough at various periods, and are mentioned
by many authors. La Colombière* speaks of two
rival courtesans who, from motives of jealousy, fought
it out with swords on a Parisian boulevard; while
Tallemant des Réaux mentions sundry swordswomen
and female rufflers who were famous in his own life-
time—amongst others Mme. de Château-Gay, "a fair
and gallant lady, who was accustomed to send cartels

---

minute investigations on this point in the British Museum.
   See also *History of Duelling*, by J. C. MELLINGEN, M.D.,
F.R.S., 2 vols., 8vo, London, 1841.

* About the year 1640 there were in Provence "two
young ladies who, abandoning the pleasures and politeness
of their sex, fought a duel with the sword only, and gave
each other several wounds. A like thing happened in Paris
five or six years ago between two ladies of pleasure of considerable attractions, who fought with short swords on the
boulevard de la Porte Saint-Antoine, and wounded each
other several times in the face and on the bosom, to which
parts the hatred and jealousy they felt towards one another
made them aim most of their blows. Two years afterwards,
when on an expedition into the country with seven or eight
of my friends, we met one of these women in a garden, who
being asked to do so by one of the chief personages of the
company present, who was of her acquaintance, told us
with no little wit and spirit the story of the duel, and lifting her neckerchief showed us a wound she had received
on the side of her right breast."—VULSON DE LA COLOM-
BIERE, *Théâtre d'honneur et de la chevalerie* (Theatre of
Honor and Chivalry).

to her lovers"; her sister, of an equally roistering
temper, whose delight was to pass her leisure time in
snuffing candles with an arquebus;* Mme. de Samois,
"who was fain to fight a duel in every field corner,"
and Mme. de Saint-Balmont, who was never without a
sword at her side, and was reputed to have taken or
killed more than four hundred men.† The same author

---

* "There were two sisters living in Auvergne, both of them
gallant ladies.   The one, who was married to a M. de
Château-Gay, of Murat, was both gallant and handsome; she
was generally to be seen on horseback, wearing huge top-
boots, kilted skirts and a man's wide-brimmed hat with
steel trimmings and feathers to crown all, sword by side
and pistols at saddle-bow.   While her husband was yet living,
M. d'Angoulême, then Comte d'Auvergne, fell in love with
her; and when he was arrested by M. d'Heurre, captain of
a private company of Light-Horse, to which this prince was
by way of showing himself ill disposed, she swore to be
avenged on this M. d'Heurre.   After she was a widow, she
had another lover named M. de Codières; he made her jealous
and she challenged him to a duel.   He accepted the challenge;
and when he began by playing the fool, she pressed him so
hard it was all he could do to master her; eventually he threw
her right on the ground and so made his peace for good and
all.   She had a grievance against certain gentlemen of her
neighborhood named MM. de Gane.   One day she met them
at the chase.   A gentleman, one of her people, and who
acted as her squire, said to her: 'Let us go back, madam; they
are three to one.'   'What matter?' she replied.   'It shall never
be said that I encountered them without attacking them.'   She
did attack them, and they were cowardly enough to kill her.
She made every possible resistance."—TALLEMANT DES
REAUX, Historiette 460; Femmes vaillantes.

† Barbe d'Ernecourt, comtesse de Saint-Balmont, born at
Neuville in 1608.—Mémoires de l'abbé Arnauld, in the "Collection Michaud et Poujoulat."

tells how a certain Mlle. Liance, having one day given Benserade, who was by way of taking liberties with her, "a great blow on the chest with her fist," at the same moment drew a short sword she always wore in her girdle and said to him, "Were you not in my own house, I would run my poniard into you."*

It only remains to name, as the last of French lady-duelists—to make no mention of those spoken of in the letters of Mme. Dunoyer—Henriette-Sylvie de Molière,† and finally Mlle. Durieux, who, Saint-Foix relates in his *Essais sur Paris*, one day attacked and fought her lover in the open street.

So it went on. It would be easy enough to cite yet other examples, down to the days of the Chevalière d'Eon, of these strange, strenuous caprices which now and again the "charming sex," prescriptively sacred for us men—shame on Diomed, who wounded Cypris!

---

* TALLEMANT DES REAUX, *Historiette* 388: *Mademoiselle Liance.*

† Mme. de Villedieu mentions a duel with swords be-tween Henriette-Sylvie de Molière and another lady. Both combatants were dressed as men.—MME. DE VILLIDIEU, *Œuvres complètés*, vol. VII.

Mme. Dunoyer speaks in her Letters of a meeting between a lady of Beaucaire and a young lady of birth, who fought with swords in a garden, and would have killed each other, had they not been separated. This duel had been, according to rule, preceded by a formal challenge.

Saint-Foix in his *Essais sur Paris* mentions a Mlle. Durieux who fought in the open street with a certain Antinotti, her lover. In 1742 a young lady of Versailles did the same.—BARBIER, *Journal.*

—would permit themselves, previous to the date when, more to be in the fashion than from any real anemic taint, they began to make an affectation of extreme delicacy.

To account for the strange attraction excercised over women by the flashing blade of a sword, one might well be tempted, over and above the various natural causes above enumerated, to seek some further occult reason, some mysterious spiritual connection between the two.

Pagan traditions point to a certain affinity, a certain kinship, existing between the weapon so highly prized and the creature so fondly loved. Pandora, first of mortal women to possess the beauty of Venus, the strength of Hercules and the courage of Mars, was, we know, the creation of Vulcan, the divine sword-maker who forged the blades the gods wielded. Out of this notion of their identity of origin was evolved in the thought of men, pondering in dreamy reverie, a sort of relationship of the sword with womankind.

There is a general resemblance between the women and the swords peculiar to each country. Both, in the Germanic and Swedish regions of the North, are as a rule large and of heavy build; both have, the one in love, the other in fencing, something ponderous and stiff about them. On the other hand, in the South of Europe, in Greece, Italy and Spain, sword and woman are alike slender and elegant, dainty in movement, and similarly decked out with gold, symbol of the sun and of the brown-haired races. The comparison may even be elaborated a step further; in Turkey, as in the East generally, in all lands where the languid Mussulman beauties of the Harem throw their limbs into listless curves and lie couched in snake-like coils, swords are mostly bent, flexible and supple as Oriental dancing-girls in their undulating postures, and like them over-loaded with gold and jewels.

The mention of these two words leads us to speak next of the dashing dames who have ever been allured by the gallant show of military pomp and luxury. All the extravagance and all the cupidity the female heart is capable of, under the strong seductions love exerts when its arrows are of gold, is displayed frankly and openly from century to century in the guise of those courtesans of the camp whose original patron deity was Venus Victrix.

From times the most remote, hordes of women were wont to follow armies in the field, devoting themselves to the life of camps and the fortunes of the Sword—always lavish of its gifts after pillage, which in turn was stimulated by the hope of carnal gratifications to follow. "A portion of the booty made by Mars in war ever goes to the profit of Priapus," is the moral appended to a certain Bithynian Fable.

The Greek warriors, for instance those who took part in the famous Retreat of the Ten Thousand, all had their *hetaerae,* or camp-ladies, the majority of whom were free-born and were attended by slave-women attached to their service, while the Lydians were accustomed to carry along with them in the field dancing-girls and flute-players to amuse their leisure. These habits of antiquity survived in the Middle ages, and a class of rapacious adventuresses, a sort of *for-lorn hope* of love, is found numerously represented in the Crusades. "The Frank soldiers," an Arab writer says, "will not go to battle, if deprived of women."

Some of these women took the Cross along with their lovers, we are told by Guibert de Nogent,* and fought in the battles against the Infidel. The Emperor Conrad was accompanied in Syria by a troop of amazons; and the letters of Pope Boniface VIII, prove that in the year 1383 a contingent of Genoese ladies, fully armed, joined in a Crusade against the Turks.†

The *galoises, donzelles and gaillardes,* (camp-girls, ladies of pleasure, wantons) of camp and field still

---

* "William, Count of Poitiers, had taken along with him a swarm of girls."—GUIBERT DE NOGENT, *Gesta Dei per Francos.* (God's Deeds by the hands of the Franks), bk. VII.

"The Monk de Vigeois, about 1180, speaking of the licence which at that time prevailed among the troops, declared he had counted in one of our armies as many as fifteen hundred concubines, whose illicit gains reached incalculable sums."— SAINTE-PALAYE, *Mémoires sur l'ancienne chevalerie* (Treatise on Ancient Chivalry), II, notes.

† Misson in his *Voyage d'Italie* (1688) says at Genoa he was shown in the small arsenal of the Palazzo-Real, or Royal Palace, a number of cuirasses and helmets for women, which he was told had belonged to certain Genoese ladies who in 1301 joined a Crusade against the Turks.

In confirmation of this and proving the accuracy of his statement, Misson quotes three letters from Pope Boniface VIII (preserved among the archives of Genoa) where much is said as to the warlike infatuation of these ladies.

figure as late as the fifteenth and sixteenth centuries in the train of warlike princes; in France they even formed a part of the household under the title of "the Royal filles de joie," and were originally under the care of the "king of the gallants," who held the rank of Captain.

During the occupation of Saint-Denis, the Maid of Orleans broke her famous sword of Fierbois striking with the flat of its blade one of the camp-girls that followed her soldiers. I mention the fact in connection with this part of my subject only as showing both the muscular vigor and the pure morality of the Virgin of Domrémy.

Later still, the *garces militaires* (soldier's wenches) were known as "ladies of pleasure following the court," in other words, following the Sword. On May-day, sacred to lovers and the budding year, they were wont to present the king with a bouquet as a Springtime Valentine.*

In war, these "merry maidens," not being subject to capture, paid no ransom and met with general consideration. They displayed the greatest luxury, "wearing jewels, dress, attire and other ornaments forbidden to other votaries of pleasure"—surely an alluring privilege for any daughter of Eve, even amongst the ranks of *honest women!*

---

* "My Lord Saint Valentine, patron saint of lovers."— MARTIAL D'AUVERGNE, *Arresta Amorum.* See also with reference to St. Valentine's day note I, p. 20, of SIR WALTER SCOTT'S "Fair Maid of Perth."

Occasionally, too, they actually followed the troops when the latter took the field. Accompanying the army of the Duke of Alva in Flanders were to be seen "four hundred mounted courtesans, fair and gallant as princesses, and eight hundred afoot as well, very well appointed." There were eight hundred present with Strossi's forces, about 1578.*

To restrain the follies the attraction of such a life led women to commit, an edict was published in 1516 to this effect: "Any woman quitting her husband and following in man's clothes and adulterously after men-at-arms, shall be beaten naked, with rods, through the town."† In spite of all this the boldest spirits "went afield and scoured the country-side in company with their *gallants,* or lovers; whilst others again fell to the lure of various popular ballads of the day. One of these rhymed catches tells how a noble captain carries off his lady love, and dresses her all in white satin at the first town he comes to; at the second, he decks her in still braver attire; finally at the third town, he *clothes her in gold and diamonds.* And "so handsome was

---

* "M. de Strossi, albeit extraordinarily strict, as indeed he had sufficiently manifested by ordering eight hundred 'filles de joie' that followed his camp to be thrown into the river Loire."—VARILLAS, *Histoire de Henry III,* vol. III.

† "For having quitted her husband and followed after men-at-arms, in man's clothes and adulterously (according to the terms of the edict of the Court of Parliament of June 20, 1515), the said woman was condemned to be beaten naked, with rods, on a market day, through the public streets of the town."

she, she passed for queen in the regiment," adds the
last couplet—surely well adapted to wake ambitious
dreams in feminine bosoms.

In Turkey as in all parts of the East where sentiment
reigns paramount, and even in France itself, where
Dunois' sword "was reckoned worth 20,000 gold
crowns, for it was mounted with rich jeweled work,"
arms of parade, personal symbols of a soldier's importance and nobility, were enriched with every adornment
of gold and precious stones. There were jewels to the
value of 225,000 livres on the hilt of the *kandjar* carried by Ali-beg, while "the Duc d'Epernon, on days of
state, wore a sword mounted with eighteen hundred
diamonds." Easy to guess how ladies encouraged such
extravagances, which were after all merely a means of
giving expression to the wish to please them, and which
served to excuse their own exorbitant toilet expenses
"in pearls, precious stones, robes of cloth of gold and
silver." Thus the innate prodigality of the Sword, exaggerated by the spirit of gallantry, tended in every way
to women's advantage, and the rich plunder soldiers
won was either wasted to gratify feminine caprice or
came eventually into feminine hands in the form of
lavish presents.

"Courage, comrades!" a Captain of the sixteenth
century cries to his men, "before long time I will set
you measuring velvet with your pikes as ell-wands,"*
—a fascinating phrase it is easy to guess the meaning of.

---

* BRANTOME, *Grands Capitaines*: M. de Salvoyson.

CHAPTER VI

SEDUCTIVE QUALITIES OF SOLDIERS VS.
MEN OF LETTERS — FEUDAL LORDS
AND THEIR RIGHTS

The better to bring out all the powers of seduction which the sword and its prestige exercised in old days over women's minds, it is needful to display, in contrast with it, the different aspects of ill-will and hostility assumed by its younger sister, the gown.

To go back to the origin of the lawyer's gown. It proceeds in the order of social evolution from the *toga,* chosen costume of the ancient Latin magistrates.

Under the primitive political organization of barbarous nations, every man was by necessary obligation a fighter, including even the priest; the gown as a symbol of special functions only began to play its distinctive part at a comparatively late period.

It was in the heart and center of Europe, towards the end of the Middle Ages, that as a consequence of the multiplication of universities and their growing importance, it began to display its various aspects to best advantage.

The old Scandinavian and Teutonic world, exclusively warlike in its original constitution, was composed of two classes and two classes only—the two sexes, under the general names of "Sword, and Distaff." But later, when the civilization of the North had reached a certain point in its development, the Sword tolerated the special functions and privileges of *clerks* and legists. Hence the origin of the *tiers état* (the Third Estate) of 1310, and the starting point of the castes and classes of modern life.

At first the chief posts appertaining to the priestly gown were invariably coveted by the military aristoc-racy,* and so arose the high clergy of the days of chivalry, ever thirsting after rich bishoprics. Under Charlemagne, the bishops† were soldiers, and long subsequently to his date abbots and even monks were still trained in the practice of arms. The Apostles themselves had to some extent been swordsmen,‡ and

---

* "When the warlike nobility saw the honors and riches there were in the Episcopate, they laid hands on it. Chiefs who lived by the sword and never left off their armor, were little likely to bend to the idea of a power stripped of arms. They entered the church with their arms and their old habits; they took with them there the life of camps."—OZANAM, *Germans before Christianity.*

† "In 803, at the assembly of Worms, a petition was presented to Charlemagne, begging that the Bishops should not be compelled to go to the wars."—OZNAM, *Civilization among the Frank^.*

‡ Some of the Apostles wore swords.—ST. LUKE, XXII, 36. —GIOTRUS, VI.

In the Garden of the Mount of Olives, "Jesus turned his thoughts to means of defence and spoke of swords. There were two among the band. Enough, said our Lord. He did not follow up the thought in any overt act."—RENAN, *Vie de Jésus.*

St. Peter resigned only one of the two swords he bore.*

After this half warlike, half religious, state of things had lasted a very considerable time, the masculine world at length split definitely into two sections— a separation recognized in the Laws of Saxony, or *Sachsenspiegel*.† Then the flower of the lowborn classes, bedizened in the mongrel costume which has nothing whether of the robe of chivalry or of the short soldier's cloak, rallies under the sign of the "temporal sword," the sword of justice. But this down to the sixteenth century continues to be habitually dominated by the Sword in Council of State.

In antiquity *hetaerae,* courtesans, whether from vitiated taste or simply as wishing to set the world talking of them, compromised some famous men of the gown, some philosophers, paltry, pretentious or cynical. Certain of them took as lovers writers, like Gorgias or Apollodorus,‡ or orators like Hyperides, masters of the eloquence that thrills mankind. The latter, their sen- sual nature stirred by their fair clients, would make speeches in panegyric of their charms or defend them before the court of Areopagus against the accusations

---

* The Law of Suabia declares that "St. Peter receives of God the two swords; he keeps for himself the sword ec- clesiastical, and hands over the temporal sword to the Emperor."—*Epist. Schwert.*—OZANAM, *Germanic Studies,* vol. II.

† Laws of Saxony,—the *Sachsenspiegel*—recognize the separation of the two powers.—*Epist. Ludovici II ad Basilis- cum imperatorem* (Letter of Louis II, to the Emperor Basil.)

‡ Apollodorus wrote a treatise on *Courtesans.*

of Demosthenes. All this is quite true, but it does not prove that the Gown has ever been able, since the gods of Greece fell, in open gallantry to enter into serious rivalry with the Sword.

Quid pluma levius? . . . *Mulier. Quid muliere?* *Nihil* (What is lighter than a feather? A woman. What is lighter than a woman? Nothing), is the phrase found in Latin satire. It means nothing more nor less than this: women have always hated morality and seriousness, precise knowledge and deliberate wisdom, which in their eyes are merely silly and hypocritical pretentions that mark the class of professional phrase-mongers.

Indeed for women the Gown, that triumph of muscular indolence, that sexual anomaly as monstrous as the dragon born of the embraces of Mars and Venus —the Gown, whence springs the type of creatures that tear each other to pieces with tongue and pen— the Gown, that has ever been pedantic and inquisitorial, forever putting awkward questions and making spiteful epigrams, systematically using a jargon unintelligible in style and diction to plain folk, could not but, if looked at in this light (and precisely in this light women have always looked at it), be absolutely antipathetic to their whole nature. All disadvantages then being on the side of the Gown, and just the opposite, all the pleasures and delightful follies on that of the Sword, it is easy to explain how the frivolous sex was bound vastly to prefer the latter. Nay! more, this preference could readily be justified simply and solely on the ground of attacks, vexations and abuse for which ladies, courtesans and good wives alike, have always had to thank the moralists and other canting personages of the long-robed kind, whom they would treat with open scorn in face of the Sword.

From the first origin of the Gown in ancient times down to the just-past days of our modern philosophers, every man capable of observing has let fly at women some vindictive epigram, or at any rate once in a way in his writings has wreaked his spite on the fair sex.

Plato, exasperated against a faithless woman, develops his whole theory of beauty without once naming them. Seneca speaks of her as an animal devoid of shame;* a doctor of the church, the prudish Origen, suppressed her altogether in the after life as being both useless and dangerous; another pedant had yet earlier declared her to be a *nocivum genus* (noxious kind); still another, following St. Paul who called her an instrument of the devil, describes her as possessed of the Evil One; lastly, in the sixth century, a particularly fine specimen of the narrow-minded pedant, a speaker at the Council of Mâcon, tried to prove that women have no souls.† Judge to what lengths "the

---

* Seneca, *De Constantia sapiente* (Of a Wise Constancy), XV, 10, 4.

† "In the sixth century, at the Council of Mâcon, a Priest was for proving that women formed no part of the human species. The Assembly voted on this thesis; and woman owed it only to a very slender majority that she was not declared to hold a place mid-way between man and beast."— Gregory of Tours.

hypocrisy and spitefulness of churchmen," (this is the
expression employed by the Queen of Navarre in one
of her tales) would have proceeded, if women had
not struck out the idea of claiming protection from the
Sword, in accordance with the elementary principles
of chivalry they imposed upon all good knights.

Pathelins, chicquanous, justiciards (Law-mongers,
pettifoggers, justicers)—such were some of the names
country-women gave formerly to the men of the long
robe, in days before magistrates had learned to be
pleasant and courteous—satirical writers with a grievance, like Jacques Olivier;* preachers seeking success
and notoriety by broad sermons; men like the brothers
Etienne,† repulsed by the wives of laymen; moralists

At another Council, a speaker thus defined woman in general: "Woman is the gate of Hell, the pathway of iniquity,
the scorpion's bite, a noxious species (*femina janau diaboli,
via iniquitatis, scorpionis percussio, nocivum genus*)"—
Quoted by M. PAUL LACROIX (le bibliophile Jacob).

* *Le tableau des piperies des femmes mondaines* (Delinea-
tion of the Trickeries of Worldly Women), where are shown
in several histories the tricks and artifices they employ (1632).
—This curious work is by Jacques Olivier, the terrible foe of
the fair sex, author of the *Alphabet de l'imperfection et malice
des femmes* (Alphabet of Feminine Imperfection and Evil-
doing).

† *Remontrance aux dames sur leurs ornements dissolus*
(Remonstrance addressed to Ladies on their Dissolute Apparel), by Brother ANTOINE-ETIENNE, Minorite, 1585.

Fra Bernardino da Feltro had preached the preceding year
at Brescia, and had caused to be publicly burned on the
Great Square those *dead locks* which all women put in all
fashions on their heads, and which they are in the habit of
wearing in order to increase their native beauty. Other vain

in whom compulsory continence has produced a morbid irritation of the brain, prosecutors, hard-faced judges, all inveigh with unseemly violence and foul words against luxury, dancing, exposing the bosom, love itself, rail at courtesans, persecute and torture tender criminals, burn witches, flagellate devotees, and have female sinners beaten with rods—all so contrary to the law dictated by the gentle wisdom of the Hindoos, "Had she a thousand faults, never strike a woman, not so much as with a flower."

Impossible to enumerate all the grievances of women against that whole class of long-robed moralists whom their cloth embitters.   The man of the black or of any other colored gown (Monks will be treated of later on) has never had, since Abelard and Heloïse, any but very equivocal successes in gallantry, successes but occasional and merely of the senses.

The paramount merit of men of the robe in the eyes of women was this: they showed themselves not hard to please where plain or passé women were concerned. Yet in spite of this excellent trait, wind-falls for the Gown, with its stern seriousness forming such a contrast to the gay successes of the light-hearted Sword, hardly ever occurred except with recluses or ardent persons of low rank, with women bent on blackmail, ill-balanced matrons or erotic old-maids.   Only the most important and richest of the gloomy and dissolute crew were now and again admitted to surreptitious

feminine ornaments likewise he had burned.—BANDELLO, Tenth Part, Third Novella.

favors by noble ladies in the superfluity of their naughtiness, or by wealthy citizens' wives and similar hypocritical and sham pious dames. Of these there were always some who wished to taste, as Tartuffe proposed, of "love without scandal and pleasure without risk," the keeping up of appearances being, according to Ignatius Loyola, in the very first rank of virtues.

The last named holy man brings us to speak of the Monks, the constant objects of ridicule on the part of their fellows of the gown, the men of letters, a jealous folk in strict accord with the spirit of their cloth.

The monks, these free-lances of an enforced chastity, fully recognized the disabilities of the religious habit as contrasted with the happy licence of the Sword, writing the while their "Champion des Dames," their "Blason des Folles Amours" (The Ladies' Champion; Heraldry of Gallant Intrigue) and a particularly filthy work on *the remedy of sinfulness,** disguise as far as may be the shape and appearance of the plain habit they wear. To follow the words of sundry Fathers of the Church, first of all they draw in their robe tight at the hips and even in other localities, then with well-polished shoes† and gloves, "they have the

---

* *La Somme des Péchés et le Remède d'iceux* (The Summary of Sins and the Remedy of the same), printed at Lyons by Charles Pesnot, about 1584, 4to. A book of filthiness composed by JEAN BENEDICTI, a Franciscan of Brittany.

† Some monks of the Middle Ages displayed these ridiculous affections even in their foot-gear. Their shoes, made much too small, were adorned with a long point and two ears, and always coated with the most shiny polish, which

look of merry-andrews more than of monks." At any
rate such was the complaint in the year 972 of Raoul,
Abbot of Saint-Rémi. Later on, and the custom was to
continue in vogue as late as 1780 for court abbés, they
wear the sword,* and this mainly to please the ladies.
"This is done," Matthew Paris assures us, "by very
amiable prelates and even by the inferior clergy."
Some of the latter used to fight duels and understood
the management of the broad-sword, the weapon which
was so dexterously wielded by Brother Bernard de
Montgaillard,† a man of rank and a member of the

---

special servants were charged with the duty of renewing
constantly.—*Réforme du Primat, ou Synode du Mont Notre-
Dame,* by RICHER, II, p. 39.

"The *Capitularies* of Charlemagne allowed monks to wear
gloves."—MENAGE, *Etymologies de la langue française,* Ghent.

* In a Novella by an unknown author, appended to the
Decameron of Boccaccio by the Giunti and Aldi, we find
mentioned as quite a usual habit on the part of a monk
towards the end of the fifteenth century, that of wearing a
sword: ". . . *E primisegli nella scarcella e tolse una spada ed
usci fuori.*" (And he put them back in his purse, and took
a sword and went out.)

STRAPAROLA (in his *Nuits facétieuses*—Comic Nights—
Thirteenth Night, Tale XI) relating how a Curé, going at
night to visit a woman, disguises himself as a swordsman,
says, "Next comes up a young man bearing in his right hand
a sword and in his left a round buckler. . . . This young
warrior, who was no other than the Curé of the village, who
was her lover and kept her as his mistress, quitting sword
and buckler, ran forward to kiss and greet her."

† Brother Bernard de Montgaillard; nicknamed *the Little*
Feuillant (Monk of the order of St. Bernard), was a skilful
fencer with the broadsword; on the occasion of the proces-

famous "League." It was a priest, "who was a master of the craft," that instructed Baron des Guerres, in view of his duel with the Sieur de Fandilles, to use a half-sword, as Brantôme, always precise in details, relates.*

From the Roman times, then, the Gown has been the distinctive garb of magistrates, as well as of the learned or industrious citizens, this class always representing merely gravity and solemnity in the eyes of women.

The fair rebels, once under the gallant and open-handed protection of the Sword, defied sumptuary edicts one and all. As for reprimands, these were

---

sion, or *show-Sunday*, of the "Leaguers" which took place at Paris on Sunday, June 3rd, 1590, he made himself conspicuous by his swordsman's tricks.

"He it was," says M. de Thou, "who animated this masquerade, showing off his broadsword play, now at the head, now at the rear, of the monkish infantry."—Notes to p. 50, of Vol. I.—L'ESTOILE, *Journal de Henri IV.*

"It was on the Bridge of Notre-Dame that the Legate reviewed, on June 3rd, 1590, the famous procession of the "League." This ecclesiastical infantry, composed of Capuchins, Carmelites, Franciscans, Reformed Franciscans, Jacobins and Feuillants, all with gown tucked up and hood lowered, helmet on head, hauberk on back, dagger by side and gun on shoulder, defiled past four abreast, having at the head the Bishop of Senlis, and for Sergeant-Majors the Curés of Saint-Jacques-la-Boucherie and Saint-Cosme. Some of these men-at-arms, forgetting their guns were loaded with ball, and wishing to salute the Legate, killed one of his Almoners at his side. His Eminence finding the review rather warm, promptly gave his blessing and retired."—*Almanach du Voyageur à Paris* (Diary of a Traveller at Paris), 1783.

* BRANTOME, *Discours sur les duels* (Treatise on Duels).

simply thrown away, contempt for everything in the
way of remonstrance being a prerogative of the sex.

By its pedantic morality and silly, simple-minded
affectations of superiority, that gave it the sorriest
mien, and even more by its inveterate habit of petty
worrying, the Gown provoked many domestic ills,
women being more often than not in search of a
matrimonial grievance to excuse their avenging themselves by some act of unfaithfulness. Such misunder-
standings the Sword was always able to turn to its
own advantage with the envious-hearted matrons of
the Gown, who in accordance with decrees they could
not elude were expressly forbidden* the luxurious ap-
pointments of noble-born wantons.

Such is a brief summary of the reasons for the ill
success in former days of the men of the long robe
strictly so called. As for the men of the pen, writers of
all sorts and poets, who not belonging to the *noblesse*
must consequently count among *gownsmen,* they were
but ill suited to the humor of the ladies, who pretty
nearly all preferred a captivating boldness of address
and amiable violence. The fact is they were far too un-
enterprising, far too stiff and awkward, too self-distrust-
ful and self-restrained, "forgetful of how a man must
demean himself with such bold, merry, stout-hearted
dames, well-knit and stalwart." They represented

---

* Wives of lawyers and citizens in general were not allowed
to wear dresses of velvet or silk "like dames and demoiselles
of high estate."—LEBER, *Pieces relatives à l'Histoire de
Frances* (Extracts relating to the History of France).

that feeling of respect which in conjunction with virtue creates fair beings to inspire their books or sonnets, herein resembling Don Quixote, who preferred to go on thinking the vizor of his helmet was sound to trying whether it actually were so. After all, the most clear-sighted women could not well help saying amongst themselves: "what good do we get out of the triumphs of their wit or their science? What good do we get out of their fame? It is merely a rival to our attractions." Petrarch refused to wed Laura.* A fine part truly, to be the mistress of Dante or the helpmeet of Galileo; to have nothing better than such visionaries to deceive! Dreamers, so ridiculous in the married state, had many faults; they were too much given to star-gazing, and above all they were far too chary in getting killed—so thought the fickle sex. There has been, so Ménage affirms,† in modern times but one single poet killed in battle, and that was only by a stone; and "the Muses," as Buchanan puts it, "are virgins because they are poor." Poverty was always, in the eyes of women, the greatest fault in men of genius and dealers in intellectual wares.

---

* Petrarch refused to marry Laura.—CHATEAUBRIAND, *English Literature*, vol. I.

The Pope offered to secularize Petrarch, that he might be able to marry Laura. Petrarch replied to this proposition of his Holiness: "I have yet many sonnets to make."

† "I know not among the moderns," says Ménage, "any other poets slain in war but Garcilasso, restorer of Spanish poetry. He was killed in Provence by a stone, in the time of Charles V." *Menagiana.*

Apollo, Shakespeare, Marlowe, Molière, and, we may even say, the majority of the immortals of the bay-leaf crown, each and all of them loved a woman who played them false. "How many perjuries to make one faithful wife?" exclaims Shakespeare. Ovid for-saken by Corinna in favor of a Roman captain returned from the Asiatic wars, complains of seeing women prefer brawny soldiers, well stocked with plunder, to less well provided rhymesters. For these last, as for so many others of the famous dead, who have never really lived, is left in all the realm of love but a very restricted space, as narrow as is their celebrated burial place in Westminster Abbey, the *Poets' Corner.*

After such a list of deceptions and disappointments undergone by men of the gown, no need to add that the Sword likewise, which did escape ridicule, did *not* altogether escape disasters in its love affairs. Odin, Caesar, King Arthur,* the noble Jehan de Saintré and the Maréchal de Richelieu, are in legend, history, ro-mance and memoirs respectively, representatives of the countless brotherhood of the *"encornaillés"* (horned gentry), to employ the generic surname Molière con-secrated to their use. The name continued applicable from century to century, as may be readily verified, to the vast majority of great men—not to speak of

---

* "Arthur, according to the *Triades galloises,* perished obscurely in 542, in a domestic war against his nephew Medrawd (Modred), who had seduced his wife Gwenhyfar (Guinevere)." Note by M. J. Buchon in his edition of *Frois-sart's Chronicles,* Vol. I.

others.* Still in spite of all this, we must repeat, all successes in gallantry were primarily on the side of the Sword.

The creatures of the robe, jealous victims of deceit, proceeded to their vengeance slowly but surely, by sly and underhand ways, affording their wives cause to scorn them under every aspect.

As a consequence of this contemptuous feeling, some contracted a "recklessness of thought and com- pliancy of spirit, before yielding to the fatal lapse." On the contrary, noble dames who were according their favors to two or more gallants at once found an indescribable stimulant in applying their love wiles in this particular way. For the bolder spirits it had a kind of glamor of successful deceit and vigilance baffled, that kept them to the mark. Besides this— and here was the exciting part—the sword hung ever suspended over their heads. Punishment on the husband's part being summary and immediate, there was real courage and a sort of heroism, and a whole gamut of thrilling emotion into the bargain, in deceit practiced at the risk of one's life, "running more hazards and perils than does a soldier in the wars." For truly, what can be more perilous than to brave the watchful suspiciousness of "an armed cuckold?" as Brantôme has it.

---

* The list of great men deceived in love is considerable. The most cursory mental review will show that the major- ity of great men of the Sword, Laurel or Gown have been deceived by their mistresses or their wives.

The first part of the *Dames Galantes* treats amongst other things of murder due to jealousy. These were terrible, particularly in the Southern countries of Europe, which copying Eastern customs, had set up a kind of code of revenge, adopting as a guiding principle a *point of honor* that was held more sacred than life itself. In Southern lands, the especial home of jealous passion, where lovers and husbands were wont to lock up their mistresses and wives, there was no security for prowling lovers because of them. "So soon as night falls," writes Arsens de Sommerdyck,* in 1655, describing Spanish life, "no man goes abroad, because of nocturnal gallantries, in Madrid or elsewhere, without a coat of mail and *broquet,*"—that is, a round buckler.

As late as the seventeenth century, the Sword was no plaything, we see, where female falsity was involved. Even in France, where complaisant husbands are sometimes very accommodating, *vulsenades†* were common; such was the name given to the killing of a wife taken in the act of adultery. As to suspected lovers, they were usually treated as follows, and the possibility

---

* *Relation de l'Etat d'Espagne* (Account of the Condition of Spain), continuation of the *Voyage d'Espagne* (Journey in Spain), by ARSENS DE SOMMERDYCK.

† "VULSENADE, murder of a woman surprised in adultery by her husband, who kills her on the spot."—LACOMBE, *Dictionary of old French.*

"For a *vulsenade* or murder of an adulterous woman by the husband, the Capitulary laws held it enough to deprive him of his arms."

threw a poetic light over their amorous visits: "The Seigneur d'Allègre, who had got off (at the assaults on Yssoire) with an arquebus shot in the thigh, was soon after killed at night through a lady of the country, whom he was paying court to."* "Some husbands there are," says Brantôme, "who kill the lady and her cavalier both together." Thus in *his* day, as in a thousand such cases, jealousy cleared the fields and streets with pistol balls, and had scarcely anything to fear from justice.

In spite of these dreadful possibilities, the Sword differing so widely as it does from the Gown in virtue of its prestige, its trappings all glittering with gold, and its other allurements, "gathers all the fairest blossoms of the garden," to use an old polite phrase of gallantry. For the gilded rapiers, for the bold spirits women and fortune smile on, are reserved the glance of challenging eyes, the provocative wiles, so full of good-will and ill thoughts.

The most enticing blades have in all ages provoked susceptible hearts among so-called virtuous wives, who yet love to do wrong in thought, to commit an unfaithfulness of the fancy, an adultery of the imagination—the abortive and unavowed bigamy so well delineated by Saint-Evrémond.†

The fact is, women would only consent to be compromised, and as we should express it nowadays dis-

---

* PIERRE DE L'ESTOILE, *Journal*, May 28, 1577.

† SAINT-EVREMOND. *Œuvres meslées* (Miscellaneous Works), Paris, 1668.

honored, by the Sword, which is the very essence of audacious enterprise and makes all offences forgiven, including its peremptory and unconventional caresses. This was originally, it would appear—before the authorities had invented the demure *rosière*—a prin-ciple very generally adopted by the mass of women. Indeed, the feudal *droit de Seigneur** (right of the feudal lord), formerly known as "poaching," was so

---

* The *Droit de Seigneur* (Right of the Feudal Lord). As to this curious custom we will quote a document of 1588, "Right over the houses of the Village of Aas."

"*Item,* when any women of the above named houses shall come to marry, the husbands before knowing their wives shall be held bound to offer them for the first night to the aforesaid Seigneur de Louvie to do with them as he will at his good pleasure, or otherwise they shall pay him a tribute.

"*Item,* if they come to have any child, they are held bound to bring a certain sum of deniers, and if it happen that it be a male child, it is free, because that it may be begotten of the efforts of the aforesaid Seigneur de Louvie the first night of *his above-mentioned pleasures.*"

In a second document taken from the *enumeration* of the Seigneur de Bizanos, of the 12th of September, 1674, we read:

"*Item,* in past times the said subjects were in such sub-jection that the predecessors of the said enumerator had the right every time and always that they took a wife in mar-riage, to lie with the bride on the night next following the wedding. This duty has, however, been converted by his aforesaid predecessors into the payment of an impost in kind."
—HENRI MARTIN, *History of France,* Appendix, vol. V.

"A parcel of ground is granted to René and his descen-dants on condition that the younger daughter shall be held bound to pay satisfaction to the Seigneur,—under honor-able circumstances and in a private chamber."—Charter of the fifteenth century in the French "*Archives Nationales.*"

far from being displeasing to newly married wives that during a period of several centuries not a single Lucretia was ever found. In those days, when folk saw a pretty woman in an interesting condition, they would say, "The Lord has passed this way," as if to thank Heaven for it. The plain ones scorned by the great men on their marriage day, merely paid their tithe tearfully at the Château. "There are girls," says Brantôme, "who do not readily give themselves to any but the Seigneurs."

The maids of Brescia whom Bayard so chivalrously respected were doubtless deeply humiliated by the incident. This act of scrupulosity dates 1512. About 1650, "The prince, who was returning drunk from Saint-Cloud, encountering pretty Mme. d'Esquevilly,* whose coach had just broken down, and finding her much to his taste, took her and led her into the wood; his courtiers each provided himself with one of the charmers who accompanied her." With due variation of scenery and actors, such an escapade is representative of every period, and no doubt women's high jinks with men of rank in former days is at the bottom of many hereditary hatreds.

In gallantry, as in processions where church-bells and blaring trumpets and salvos of artillery saluted it, the Sword that so gaily fronts every peril and wins every heart, everywhere marched first as of proper right. Everywhere it played its lion's part with a

* TALLEMANT DES REAUX, *Historiettes*—Mme. de Champré, vol. IV.

jovial self-assertion, spiting with its splendor, its gallant mien and broad shoulders the *Cedant arma togae*
(let arms give place to the gown) of Cicero,* himself
a creature of the gown, who once had the ambition
to play the General.

Just because of its incontestable prëeminence the
Sword was always an object of hatred to the Gown,
rendered jealous and ill-natured by women, the everlasting source of discord and greed. So much was
this the case that "Councillors are to be seen quitting
the gown and cap and starting out to trail the sword."†

Nevertheless, sworn foes as were the men of the
gown to the brilliant daring and haughty elegance of
the Sword, they yet contributed something, in virtue
of their official panegyrics extorted by political expedi-
ency, to its glory and even to its triumphs. Religious
differences often found their solution by its help, and
the popes, who bore it as one of the chief symbols
of their power, would despatch as a mark of deference
to famous captains a blade they had blessed. The
monastic orders again were constantly indebted to it,
and used to celebrate its victories by depositing it

---

* A verse Cicero composed in his own praise, in memory
of his Consulship.

Cedant arma togæ, concedat laurea linguae!

"Let arms give place to the gown, the laurel to the tongue."

In other words, let military power represented by the
sword make way for civil power represented by the toga.
This latter was at Rome what we call amongst ourselves the
bourgeois costume.

† BRANTOME, *Vies des Grands Capitaines* (Lives of Great
Captains), M. de TAVANNES.

on their high altars,* absolving its crimes and granting its heroes stately obsequies. Jurists terming themselves *doctors in dueling* published its laws and its uncodified points of honor; while historians and orators recorded and extolled its prowess, and poets ever officious in its service wrote sonnets they devoted to the use of love-sick soldiers who could not spell. Desportes in 1570 earned at this trade with the Duc d'Anjou an income of better than thirty thousand livres.†

---

* "In our days (thirteenth century) aspirants to the profession of arms take the sword from off the altar."—PIERRE DE BLOIS.

Previously to the Roman conquest, the priests were accustomed to arm the Saxon warriors.

† The Duc d'Anjou "employed the Muse of Desportes to tell his love to Renée de Rioux (the Fair Lady of Châteauneuf), and this traffic in gallantry brought the poet in thirty thousand livres a year."

Tallemant des Réaux says of M. de Montmorency: "He was brave, rich, gallant and generous, danced well, rode well, and had always in his pay men of letters, who made verses for him."—TALLEMANT DES REAUX, II.

CHAPTER VII

DEBAUCHERY DURING THE CRUSADES — CHIVALRY MODIFIED BY ORIENTAL PASSIONS

Women always, as Montaigne observes, "wielding great power over men have ever, from age to age, determined under its different characters the bearing and typical aspect of the Sword." These different characters may, subsequently to heroic times, be classified according to four distinct periods: those of the Knight, the Gallant, the Cavalier, and the Man of Pleasure, respectively.

We took in the first place as starting point the iron age—iron and the loadstone having been held representative of Mars and Venus in the mysteries of the tender goddess. Now, however, it behooves us in the interests of clearness not to go quite so far back into the past. The age of revival having given the warrior fresh vigor and woman a second maidenhood, it will suffice for our purpose if we begin with those centuries in which we find the Sword in its pure devotion exalted by the supremest chastity, in other words the centuries of nascent chivalry.

From the lily's heart, symbol of woman in her highest purity, had emanated sundry simple-hearted beliefs. The Virgin claimed this trusting faith, and lo! Saint

Deïcola* without a shadow of hesitation hung his cloak on a sunbeam.

These beliefs, this boundless credulity it was which, six centuries later, determined the form taken by the chivalric ideal in love and religion.

Before the ecstasies of Christianity the martial spirit of the ancient world grew obsolete; accordingly military enthusiasm became metaphysical, then sentimental, then presently devoted itself out and out to the service of woman, once again erected into a Divinity.

Thus we find the warrior regenerated, his sword of truest steel forming with its cross-hilt an emblem of faith, and woman at the same time emancipated from her so-called original sin. Under these novel conditions love is destined to blossom forth, purified of every stain, and provoke all ecstasies of respect and adoration. Thus the epoch of chivalry and knightly honor shapes itself, with its long succession of mystical Sir Galahads.

For a brief while a glimpse is half seen of a perfect world, actors and scenery alike above reproach. But it was of very short duration; the ideals of purity and holiness which Christianity had set up, utilizing to this end the hysterical exaltation of women, were not long kept up by the fair ladies of those days, while the instinctive promptings common to them all soon resuscitated the sensuality of the ancient world. This relapse of morals is strikingly betrayed in medieval

---

* SAINT DEICOLA, see *Bollandist Lives of the Saints*, vol. II, p. 202.

times in those extravagant and exacting tasks of love that fair ladies laid upon men of the Sword, bending so submissively to their imperious will.

Taking as starting point the first commencement of chivalrous or ideal love, we must pursue our inquiry into women's habits during and after its full development in the twelfth century. For without their active participation no social movement is possible or indeed conceivable.

And first of all this main fact must be clearly grasped, viz., that it is from this new power which women had acquired that proceed by an obvious course of evolution the gradually perfected laws of chivalry. The proof lies in their general drift and tenor, corresponding exactly as they do in spirit with the rules formulated in the "tribunals and parliaments of gentle bearing." In these courts would all the choicest ladies of the land hold forth on knotty points, degrees of offence and "cases of love," regulating the subjection of the Sword and granting their tenderest favors, "above and beyond the free giving of the mouth and the hands."* It is to be noted that these favors in accordance with the formulated rules could be legitimately conceded, up to and including the very last but one. After this penultimate selfsurrender known as the "petite joie," or *minor gratification†* nothing else

---

* In the Rules of Love, as formulated in the days of chivalry, rules dictated by the ladies, we find they had admitted the practice of granting as an incitement to their knights the freedom of mouth and hands.

† "Petite oye," or petite joie (minor gratification)—favor

was left but the final "solacement of Venus"; and the fair ladies of rank reserved nothing of their persons in-tact—"except the rest." In such complaisant wise did sensuality gently temper idealism under the deceptive guise of the most transparent virtue.

Such carnal concessions once admitted in the politics of sentiment, the strangest complications followed. For instance, in certain cases, the lady mistresses of the castle "would not have been able to sleep," till they had equipped with one of their serving-women the couch of the knight enjoying the hospitality of their demesne.* Further commentary is needless.

In spite of these drawbacks to a high morality, all questions of honorable bearing were under the general sanction of female authority. The latter made no attempt at concealment, but boldly exhibited its pre-tensions and claims in such terms as these:

"All valiant and true knights shall honor the ladies, shall not suffer to hear them evilly spoken of; for of them, after God (so adds the original formula), comes

---

of ladies: "All favors this side of the last and final."— MENAGE, *Etymologies of the French Language*, under "Petite Oye."

"The title *petite oie* is given, in shameful traffic, to such criminal liberties as a man takes with a woman, when they do not extend to the last excess; the familiarities and smaller favors a man may obtain from a woman, when he cannot have the last and final."—TREVOUX, *General Dictionary of the French Language*, under *Oie.*

* "A Lady who welcomes a knight in her house cannot go to sleep without sending him one of her women to keep him company."—*Fabliaux*, MSS. du Roi, No. 7715, fol. 210 verso, col. I.

the honor which men win." Whosoever doth out'
rage them, shall be declared recreant by the voice of a
herald-at-arms.* Somewhat later it was decreed at
the sittings of the Provençal Courts of Chivalry to
this effect: "The duty of a knight is to please us, to
make us happy in all good ways, and *to be discreet.*"
This last recommendation is not very discreet itself,
and opens a door to a good many suppositions. In
Germany, landgravines and dames of rank were ac'
customed, as sovereign ladies, to be courteously dis'
robed and put to bed by their lovers;† after this, com'
mon politeness bound the latter to reticence.

Their system of absolutism, based by women on the
power of their carnal attractions, allowed their caprice
to far outrun the limits of the possible. A fair lady,—
even an unknown one,—could, among other extrava'
gant behests, despatch an admirer otherwise unoccupied
to go bring her a mantle fringed with "the beards of
nine conquered kings."‡ Such extravagances were
admitted by the principles of chivalry, "an institution
sane enough at its origin, but run mad before its end."

---

* CORNELIUS AGRIPPA, *Paradoxe sur l'incertitude, vanité et
abus des sciences* (Paradox concerning the Uncertainty, Van'
ity and Abuse of the Sciences), 1582, Paris, Jean Durand.

† DR. JOHANNES SCHERR, *Society and Manners in Ger'
many,* 1st part, ch. V.; *Chivalry at Court.*

‡ In the *Chevalier aux ij espées* (Knight with the two
Swords), a MS. preserved in the National Library of France,
a lady requires of King Ris to give her a mantle fringed with
the beards of nine conquered kings, and hemmed with the
beard of King Arthur who was yet to be conquered. The
mantle was to have "the tassel likewise of his beard."

On studying the usages of chivalry, we find first of
all that the feats of arms and *emprises* of the old
Paladins, actions stimulated by some waving *favor,**
such for instance as a garment of the loved one,† show
the same character of enthusiasm as that originated by
St. Theresa, that is to say, all the fanatic fervor of a
passion-fraught and disordered brain that is firmly
persuaded it has a sacred mission to perform.

While to please their ladies the simple-minded fire-
eaters, the collar of their servitude round their necks,
go forth as knights-errant to pick quarrels anywhere

---

* *Frauengünste* or woman's favor.

"When the knights of past ages used to travel through
foreign kingdoms to prove their valor, they were wont to
carry some favor of their mistresses, to wit scarfs, bracelets,
ribbons, muffs, girdles, plumes and diamond ornaments, and
other gawds, which they would give them and themselves
fasten on some conspicuous part of their person. These
gracious presents they called *emprises of love,* wishing to
give it to be understood that their chief aim and enterprise,
or *emprise,* was to fight bravely for the love of those ladies
who had given them these precious pledges and stimulants
of honor."—V. DE LA COLOMBIERE, *Théâtre d'honneur et
de la chevalerie* (Theatre of Honor and Chivalry), vol. I.

† On her side the lady, well instructed, went to her
wardrobe and took a *chanise* (that is to say, a shift) which
she gave to the most trusty of her squires, bidding him on
his part to carry it to one of those three knights whom she
named to him: "Let him away at once to the tourney, and
if he is willing to live and die in my service," she said to
him, "as he has promised me, let him don this *chanise* by way
of cuirasse."—SAINTE-PALAYE, literal translation of an old
piece of French verse entitled: *Des trois chevaliers et de la
chanise* (Of three Knights and the Shift). Thurin MS., no.
G. I., 19.

and everywhere with passers-by, the noble beings they idolize behave in such ways as these:

In their feudal homes, where idleness was for ever whispering ill advice, the hours are all too slow in rolling by, while the insipid monotony of life with a husband, whom out of sheer caprice they will per-suade to hold travelers to ransom or rob them outright, or even to coin false money, eats out their hearts. Eager for excitement and pleasure, they long for fresh distractions; they crave to overleap the cramping bounds of habit, to taste unknown joys, above all to have room and freedom. Wearied of idle hours before their mirror,—still too small to reflect them from head to foot,—their imagination is already a-dreaming of the licence (that will before long be a reality) of palaces, of courts and gallant courtiers, of gay visits and merry plays in the theatres of country castles. Women are bored; the world is soon to be transformed afresh.

Then it is that tormented by desire of change, they have read to them, long before the date when they have learned to read themselves, the poems, the licentious romances, presently the obscenities of the "Tales of the Gay Science." These productions, specially written to please them, under their eyes and it may almost be said to their dictation, degraded little by little the pure, fanatic love of the golden age of chivalry.

In the days of its highest fervor, whilst strangely enough obscene figures intruded among the paintings and decorative carvings of cathedrals and abbeys, women make common cause with the monks, pursuing

unavowed and unavowable ends of their own. Both
are desirous, under pretence of religious enthusiasm,
of ridding themselves of the troublesome, jealous claims
of the idle Sword, of the strait-laced and domineering
knights who had married and ennobled them, and to
send off on foreign service "that multitude of warriors
out of work,"* whose exuberant vigor must be turned
into some, if possible, wise and useful channel. Such
were, albeit the old, conventional views of the schools
say otherwise, the veritable motives of the earliest
Crusades.

Here again as always, women gave the starting push
to the social revolution, for with them insignificant
causes sometimes had important effects. The defeat
of Pompey the Great at Pharsalia was due to the fact
that in the battle in question the cavalry of his army
consisted of young nobles, whose vanity made them
fearful, as Caesar had foreseen would be the case, of
wounds in the face. The defeat of the French at
Courtray arose from the circumstance that the City
Fathers of Bruges would not pay the extravagant expenses in dress incurred by the citizens in order to play
the dandy before the ladies. A woman destroyed the
Bastille, Michelet declares; and again only yesterday
court-ladies† imperiled the ancient Ottoman Empire

---

* "That multitude of unemployed warriors, that abundance
of a feudal force, whose only practice was found in preying
on itself, all this hurried the Christian peoples into more
than one great conquest."—VILLEMIN, *Mélanges historiques*
(Historical Miscellanies).

† According to a communication contributed to the nine-

and the general peace of almost every nation in Europe.

The inner policy of the ladies somewhere about half way through the Middle Ages may be summed up in a few words: "Let us be," they say to all simple and gallant knights; "away with you, and win us in the far lands of the Dawn precious stuffs, titles, fortune, girdles of gold work—things we every one of us crave." And lo! the nobility of Europe on the road. Verily what woman wills, God wills!

Free at last. They are virtually widows, and intoxicated with the sense of freedom. Scorning to be like

---

teenth *Siècle* from Salonica, the young Bulgarian girl who was the cause of the serious events that happened in that town, shook the Ottoman Empire and indirectly occasioned the death of Abdul-Aziz, would seem to have been anything but an interesting personality.

With regard to the part of agitators and revolutionaries played by women in the social organism, two passages from the *Figaro* (May 11, 1878) may be quoted:

"The female sex played an important rôle in this plot against the peace of Russia and of Europe. General Ignatieff, we are assured, was powerfully assisted at court by the influence of his aunt, Mme. Malzow, and by the Countess Antoinette Bloudoff. . . ."

"The Emperor Alexander, it would appear, does not attempt to hide his irritation. At a friendly evening given by the Empress, the Czar having come in and the Countess Bloudoff having asked him if there were any news, his Majesty answered: "What have you to do with it? Leave men to take care of the government; if women had not interfered so much in politics, we should not have this *cursed* war on our hands!"

The Emperor Napoleon I used to say: "Women must be nothing at my court; they will hate me, but I shall have quiet."—MME. DE REMUSAT, *Letters.*

ordinary Christians, they adopt fancy names such as Rostangue, Phanette, Yolande, Yseult, or Blanche Fleur.* They proceed, what with "the never-ending giving of love-tokens," what with "the kind bestowal of loving guerdon," to take complete possession by way of the senses of the rising generation, which is left in their sole discretion to teach and educate. Merely as a pleasing distraction they set to work to *form* shy young noblemen and half-grown pages. By the gentle compulsion of their freely given caresses that provoke a precocious fondness to too frequent familiarities, do they ruin the rising generation and from childhood pervert the whole class of gentlemen. "Impudent as a page" is the phrase the women of 1730 will cry at some boyish liberty, quite proud of the result of their work of corruption steadily pursued for so many hundreds of years.

Other striplings, having become squires on probation at fourteen† and expert far beyond their years in love matters, spread still further abroad the new fashioned ways of love and dalliance.

---

* Stephanette, Alalete, Hermyssende, Mabille, Rostangue, Bertrane and Jausserande are fond, fancy names borne by some of the ladies mentioned by André le Chapelain.—*Manuscript on the Courts of Love in the twelfth century.*

† "In the conditions of Esquire, to which youths were usually raised at the age of fourteen years, on ceasing to be pages, the young pupils came into closer contact with the persons of their lords and ladies, and were admitted with more confidence and familiarity into their friendship, etc."— SAINTE-PALAYE, *Mémoires sur l'ancienne chevalerie* (Memoirs as on the Ancient Chivalry), vol. I.

These are revealed in all their details in the old romances and metrical tales, and inevitably led to the
physical degradation of the knightly class and the decay
of all respectful belief and trust in women.

Adopting the new mode of life consequent upon
emancipation, they gave themselves up heart and soul
to pleasure, and leaving nothing more to be asked for,
accorded liberally to each aspirant the payment for his
devotion. Already, as they sit weaving "crowns of
greenery, the while some French minstrel skilled in the
craft of words, recited in their ears lays, virelays and
other minstrelsies," they quite forgot the absent,
whether lovers or husbands, who lay languishing in
captivity at Mansourah or elsewhere in Saracen lands,
waiting their long deferred ransom with sighs and tears,
as Joinville describes it.

Not one of them, should a ghost come back one day
from Palestine, will die of joy, like Ulysses' faithful
hound!

The first Crusade, "conceived without any true object or reason, that could be avowed," was as we have
just pointed out, the result of occult and hidden exciting causes, in which women took a large share. Solely
as having contributed to bring about these wars in far
off lands, where the debauched lives of the noble combatants showed how little religion had really to do with
it,* they are primarily responsible for the decay of

---

* Saint Louis lamented the fact that even quite close
to his own tent the pick of his chivalry had established
places of prostitution. Joinville tells us of the complaints

chivalry and its ideals of sentiment. In very truth, the hero adventurers of the expeditions to Palestine, their wits sharpened and their infatuation cured by distant travel, ended by buying concubines and slave-women in the bazaars of Asia, and eventually brought back from the East a fierce love of luxury and with it the most shameful of the vices of antiquity. Abominations of this sort, the same which undid the Knights Templars, was at a later date divulged in the language of the Law Courts at the trial of Gilles de Rays.* Let us pass lightly over such shameful subjects, and return to the home life of the ladies who dwelt in feudal castles.

During the long absences of husbands or of respect-ful, devoted swains—in other words, of tiresome bores—what did the fair ladies left behind do for amuse-ment? To supplement their domestic enjoyments, and coming as a pleasing diversion from without, may be named the visits of trouvères and troubadours, a class that does not figure largely in the Holy Wars. Along with other minstrels, they had right "to free entry, victual and lodging"—all of which they paid for in

---

of the king who could not succeed in suppressing these hot-beds of debauchery. On this subject may be consulted the account given by M. Fleury, p. 379 of his *Mœurs des Chré-tiens* (Manners and Customs of the Christians), of all the disorders which prevailed in the armies of the Crusades in Joinville's days.

* Trial of Gilles de Laval, better known under the name of Gilles de Rays.—Documents preserved in the National Library of France (antique collections), no. 8357. Extract published by P. L. JACOB, *Procès célèbres* (Famous Trials), Paris, 1858.

songs. These poets who sing of love in suggestive couplets, these Bohemians of a fighting age, these parasites
and flatterers,* formed an agreeable distraction when admitted into the townships, castles or strongholds of the
countryside, to which the ladies invited them that they
might contribute their free-spoken quips and cranks to
the talk and day-dreams of summer evenings.

---

* In a general way, the greater or less renown a lady
enjoyed depended on the more or less of praise she received
from the troubadours and the greater or less celebrity of
the said minstrels. The lady who was best besung was
likewise the best served in love.

These venal singers had the right of entry into all places;
their meed was food and lodging, and they paid their debts
in songs.

An English edict of the fourteenth century prescribes
certain limitations:

"Edward, by the Grace of God, etc. . . . to the Sheriffs
greeting:

Whereas, many idle persons, under color of professing
themselves to be *minstrels,* have been and are received to
drink and eat in the houses of other men, and are not content to depart without presents from the masters of the
houses; wishing to repress these disorderly proceedings and
this idleness, we have ordained that no one shall so intrude
himself, to drink and eat, into houses of Prelates, Earls and
Barons, without being a minstrel, etc.; it shall be forbidden
that more than three or four at most come there the same
day. And as regards houses of lesser quality, none shall be
suffered to enter therein without being bidden; and they
which shall be so bidden, shall be bound to content themselves with drink and meat, without making any further
demand, and if they offend against this ordinance, they shall
forfeit the rank of minstrels."—Abbé DE LA RUE, *Essai histor.
sur les bardes, les jongleurs,* etc. (Historical Essay concerning
the Bards, Jongleurs, etc.)

Formidable as their vindictive satires, which they hawked about from town to town and from castle to castle, the fair coquettes took care to wheedle them by many an unstinted concession of their favors. In this way they earned public panegyrics for themselves, directing at the same time the jongleur's biting couplets against their rivals.

Easy to picture, judging by modern notions, what an attraction and what a satisfaction to their vanity the liveliest and prettiest dames must have found in such public advertisement of their charms, in such attacks and such vengeance wreaked on their neighbors.

In such wise as a rule did the *gentilfames* (ladies of family) spend their leisure, the while their husbands and lovers were fighting or dying of the Plague in Palestine.

The profound importance, under old-time social conditions, of this line of behavior on the part of women is not difficult to comprehend

In addition to the evidence already adduced, many other proofs exist to demonstrate the fact that from its first origin which is based upon the Christian Gospels, the whole character and form of chivalry was in essence subordinated to the authority of women.

Already in classical times, the Greeks, and later on the Romans, had borrowed largely at the instigation at once of courtesans and of honorable matrons, from the customs, the luxury and the sensuality of eastern nations.

Under a like influence the Gauls, and subsequently

the Germans, adopted various usages coming originally from the same source and disseminated abroad by the Roman conquest.

Finally in the Middle Ages, simultaneously with irruptions of the Saracens into the west and above all with the settlement of the Arabs and Moors in Spain, there was displayed in the South of Europe, whence it was reflected widely over the north, a fresh infatuation on the part of womankind for the romantic modes and fancies of the passionate Orient.

From the Arabs again came the fashion of public displays of prowess and elaborate spectacles in the open air, diversions the Sword consecrated in old days to the pleasuring of noble dames and demoiselles wearied with the sameness of their lives.

The hawking parties where they loved to fly their falcons, the tourneys where on great occasions they might be seen stripping themselves garment by garment to their shifts* in their wild enthusiasm, the assaults at

---

* We read in *Perceforest*, vol. I, fol. 155, verso, col. I how at the end of a tourney "the ladies were so stripped bare of their attire that the greater part were all but naked, for they departed thence, their locks lying over their shoulders more yellow than fine gold: and beside only their coats without sleeves; for they had given everything to the knights to bedeck them withal, wimples and hoods, cloaks and shifts, sleeves and bodices. But when they did see themselves in such case, they were as it were one and all ashamed; but so soon as they did see that each and every one was in the like case, they did all set to laugh at their adventure; for that they had given away their jewels and their very clothes with such good heart to the knights, that

arms, the single-stick bouts, the jousts and last of all the "tiltings at the ring," were nothing but a complicated imitation on this side of the Pyrenees of the Mussulman *fantasias*, then in full vogue at Seville and Granada.

Already about 1300 women were ready to grant, without restriction or scruple, to such champions as served their vanity to good effect all privileges of the *merry life*, for as Bacon says, "dangers are fain to be paid in pleasures."

Hugue Brunet, one of the earliest troubadours, laments this change in the manners of his day: "I have seen the time," he says, "when a lace, a ring, a glove, was payment enough for a lover for the signs and tokens, the protestations and declarations, of fondness of a whole long year. Today it is straightway a question of granting him all and everything. . . . In those happy days that are no more, lovers were fain rather to hope for the supreme and final bliss than to win it at once." Such patience ended, as may be supposed, in tiring out that of the fair ones, and the discreet methods of these pure-souled Paladins underwent a speedy reformation at their hands. They were not long in teaching a lesson or two to such noble-hearted but simple-minded heroes.

"Men valiant in arms, of gracious and loving mien," to use Froissart's expression, the heroes of the hour

---

they did never note their stripping bare and divestment of the same."—SAINTE PELAYE, *Mémoires sur l'ancienne chevalerie* (Memories concerning ancient chivalry), vol. I, notes, 2nd part.

coveted by every female heart, the victors in tourneys who had the right to choose and proclaim before the envious crowd of rivals some one fair lady as Queen of Beauty, expected to be well recompensed by her for their act of courtesy.

There can be not doubt about it that the emancipation of morals and development of sensual licence among the military class in the Middle Ages were due more than anything else to the good pleasure of the ladies. They it was and no one else who cut short the reign of sentimental mysticism, and set up the fashion of physical love instead.

The knights of old were, whether by convention or through their own diffidence, or perhaps only in consequence of their tender fondness, far too humbly submissive to women's will to venture on the smallest act of initiative, where *their* pleasure, caprice or authority were involved. Such a thing was not to be dreamt of according to the ideas of those days.

To please the sex and win their favor was the constant preoccupation of the Sword. In all matters, from the Germans Tacitus describes onwards, this sentiment, this ideal, is predominant, still further growing in intensity during the ages of chivalry.

In those days, should a town be besieged, defenders and assailants would as a matter of course send each other challenges on days of truce, and in mere wantonness of emulation break lances in honor of the ladies, encouraged from the walls by the presence of stout and gallant dames looking anything but famished by the rigors of the siege.* These were the heart and soul for the defence no less than the bait and stimulant of the attack; and every man did his best to win or to defend them.

To set free three hundred ladies beleaguered and imperiled at the Market of Meaux, on June 9, 1358, Froissart relates,† the Comte de Foix, the Captal de Buch and the Duc d'Orleans, "slew and put to an end" that day more than seven thousand "Jacques" out of a total of nine thousand who had sallied out from Paris and the neighborhood.

This feat of arms, a perfectly authentic one, by-the-

---

* "At that spot was engaged a skirmish very close and very perilous. The combat was fought in a place well chosen for such men as were fain to distinguish themselves in arms for love of their ladies, for all the dames and demoiselles of Pontevedra looked on from the top of the rampart of the town."—GUITIERRE DIAZ DE GAMES, The Victorial: Chronicle of Don Pedro Nino, etc., 1379-1559. French Translation by the Comte de Circourt.

† Gaston, Comte de Foix, known by the surname of Phoebus, returning from the Crusade of Prussia along with the Captal (Governor) de Buch, their whole following consisting of only forty lances, attacked and dispersed 7000 of the "Jacques" (insurgent peasants) at the Market of Meaux: where had taken refuge 300 women whom the "Jacques" wished to lay hands on. "When these mischievous folk," Froissart says, who reports the whole affair, "saw them thus orderly drawn up (the horsemen, that is to say), albeit they were in exceeding small odds against themselves, they were in no way so hardy and eager as before; but the first ranks began to fall back, and the gentlemen to pursue after them. They killed thousands of them."—FROISSART, Chronicles vol. I, ch. XLVII, year 1358.

by, is by itself enough to prove the devotion of the
Sword to women,* as well as the vast superiority it
had over what was called the *foot-rabble*. It gives us a
good idea of what the heroes of chivalry, albeit no
longer in the enjoyment of their early primitive vigor,
could even yet accomplish in the hope of a guerdon of
caresses.

Throughout Europe towards the end of the Middle
Ages, the costume worn by the nobility of the Sword
becomes grotesque—again under feminine influence.
Petrarch writes in one of his letters to Pope Urban V,
in 1366, commenting on sundry habits of the day:
"Gentlemen wear their hair plaited on the neck like
some animal's tail, and drawn back on the forehead
with ivory-headed pins." Sacchetti, a few years later,
criticized in his *Novelli* the Florentine nobles who
from motives of vanity used to squeeze in their but-
tocks in hose many sizes too small for them. Such

---

* In contrast with this undoubted fact we may mention
an incident characteristic of modern times.

In 1848, Berlin had its insurrection; the city had to be
retaken from the insurgents in the same way as Paris was
recovered from the Communards in 1871.

Before commencing hostilities, the insurgents despatched
certain *parlementaires* to treat with General Wrangel. These
informed the Commander-in-Chief of the attacking troops that
at the first cannon-shot fired by him, they would hang his
wife.

The General's only answer was to open fire.

As soon as he was enabled to enter the city, he turned to
his aide-de-camp and said to him:

"I am curious to know whether they've hung my good
lady or no."

fantastic extravagances, all aiming at one and the same end, the seduction of the fair sex, are to be found in all countries, even in grave and solemn England. The fashionable world there would readily bestow its applause on anyone, man or woman, who was the first to invent a new *fad* or fashion; while the nobility of the Sword, ruined by lavish entertainments, in other words by their devotion to women, scoured the highroads to plunder the merchants' trains and so get money for their mistresses. At the same time losses at play are already described as leading to "crime, disaster and disgrace." In France, the land of light-hearted frivolity, great lords were to be seen bargaining away their castles and fiefs to Louis XI, to find wherewithal to lead a yet more festive life with their fair favorites. Such wild doings were no less rife among squires than among knights.

There is no lack of evidence to demonstrate the ill effects produced by sentimental and by sensual excesses on the physical and moral powers of fighting men.

In every period the ways and habits of the Sword have first and foremost exhibited in the highest degree the irresistible influence of the female element; which according to one modern physiologist is really and truly a negative element, a diminution, an enfeeblement of the masculine. Under this persistent influence the Sword in Europe, before the end of the ages of chivalry, fell away more and more by slow but sure stages from the heroic type displayed by the grand figures of its early days.

Military costume, as known to history from antiquity downwards, would by itself suffice to prove by the successive modifications and ridiculous fashions it underwent the fact that the dignity and character of the Sword were at all epochs subordinate to the caprices of women. First of all, in barbarous ages, it was stern and stiff in type, framed to "inspire terror" by its very look; already under Saint Louis, though he enjoined on his knights the duty of a plain and honest simplicity, it had grown rich and splendid, while after his reign it made greater and ever greater concessions as time went on to the effeminate and merely ornamental. At the bidding of the sex whose sole preoccupation is the toilette, a soldier's dress became sumptuous, and after a while indecent,—so much so as to push into the background at first sight all idea of its real object. "Suits of mail made to run away in" is the phrase made use of by the writer who continued Nangis' chronicle, speaking of the curtailed armor of the knights discomfited by the English at Crécy. The chronicler of Saint-Denis again, and at a later date Monstrelet* and the Italian author Sacchetti, have said in regard to costume every hard thing that could be said of the young men of their day.

---

* "Men took to the wearing of shorter doublets than they had done aforetime, in such wise that you could see plain the fashion of their backsides, etc., just the way you would dress up monkeys,—which was a very unfortunate and very immodest thing. They wore likewise on their doublets huge epaluets to show how broad they were of the shoulders."— MONSTRELET, Chronicles.

This degeneration may be verified merely by a study carried out in any collection of weapons of war of the gradual diminution in size and weight of the old sword-blades, and of the rapiers in the last years of all. The fighting men of primitive epochs, who could give such terrible slashing blows, had at first grown continually bigger and bigger along with their swords, called at first "one-handed," presently becoming swords "of a hand and a half." Their immediate descendants waxed stronger and ever stronger by wielding the tremendous "two-handed broadsword," of an enormous size and weight. Froissart shows us how Archibald Douglas swung this gigantic weapon with deadly effect. Eventually comes a diminution and shrinkage of all this brawny vigor, and while blades are lengthened and get thinner and thinner and more and more spit-like, we meet all through the period of the "rufflers" and swaggerers of the Sword, both in France, Italy and Spain, with the short sword, or half-sword, the *mezza espada, media espada.*

As brute strength diminishes, quickness and scientific movements taking its place in fighting, sword-blades are more and more refined, grow more and more sharp and subtle, like the point of honor they defend to the death. Fencing being now a matter of ruse and stratagem, the swordsman no longer requiring to be robust, makes agility his systematic study; while henceforward the fighter, losing his old bearings, aspires more than ever to be rid of the weight of his old-fashioned equipment. He takes Saint Drausin as his patron, who makes gallants invulnerable, and adopts for good and all the traitorous aid of arquebus and artillery. Simultaneously he strips himself of the different parts of mailed armor, rendered useless by the power of gun-powder. Eventually, clad simply in velvet or cloth, he exposes himself thus undefended in assaults and battles.

CHAPTER VIII

WOMEN TURN TO EROTIC WRITINGS — PROFESSIONAL PROSTITUTES SET AN EXAMPLE

The point at which we now take up the discussion marks the epoch when woman is finally tired of being taken as an ideal—a thing comprehensible enough in itself, if we consider how the sex almost invariably possesses an instinct of coquetry that takes umbrage as it were at a too obtrusive and too persistent respect on our part. Accordingly they were not long in trans' forming metaphysical love into quite another sort, one altogether much more prompt and ready. This trans' ference was followed so far as the Sword was concerned by the most disastrous consequences, of which the state of morals resulting from the change afford unmistakable evidence.

As a result of the public licence allowed themselves by *gentilfames*—orgies represented by the gay doings of Eleanore of Guyenne and later by those fêtes at Saint-Denis where the Queen of Sicily and Isabeau of Bavaria* met as comrades in licentiousness, the sym'

---

* "In 1339 Isabeau of Bavaria invited the Queen of Sicily, who had come to visit Paris, to make a pilgrimage to Saint' Denis. This fête, tournament of arms and festivities lasted three days, and finished up, so say the chronicles of the time, with a masquerade and nocturnal orgy during which the

pathies of the lower classes already show a tendency to desert the Sword; while on the part of the latter the old respectful love towards women is notably enfeebled, as was their own good pleasure it should be.

Whilst these latter are exposing themselves "with breasts all bare in public, and addressing their suppli-cations to my lord Asmodeus, the alluring demon of luxurious living," high morality and good manners alike decay, and Messieur Geoffrey La Tour Landry, who used to mark with chalk the doors of ladies of ill repute,* is like the pure-souled Bayard, merely a last, out-of-date survival of the old chivalric ideas.

From these days of decadence dates the common use

---

highest ladies, the queen included, surrendered themselves to men whom they did not know. The Monk of Saint-Denis, after giving a description of this fête, adds; "Everyone strove to satisfy his passions thereat; and we have said all when we say there were husbands who profited by the wicked behavior of their wives, and maids likewise who lost all heed for their honor."—*History of Saint-Denis*, ch. VII.

"And it was matter of common report (it is a question of certain fêtes given under Charles VI), that the said jousts did end in disgraceful doings in matter of love intrigues, whereof many evils have since arisen."—JUVENAL DES URSINS, *History of Charles VI*.

* The Chevalier Geoffrey La Tour Landry, a gentleman of Anjou, in a paper of instructions addressed to his daugh-ters about the year 1370, mentions a knight who was accus-tomed to mark with white crosses and marks of infamy the door of mansions inhabited by ladies of doubtful morality.

The outspoken phraseology of the document mentioned gives a measure of the licence permitted in language supposed to be fit for women and practiced with girls in this epoch, already deeply corrupt.

of the finical word *gentilhomme* (gentleman, gentle man), an expression of purely feminine formation which by degrees superseded as a designation of the man of the Sword the earlier title of *chevalier,* or knight. 'And so," a document of 1490 informs us, "ladies nowadays say a *gentleman,* no longer a *knight;* speaking of their friend, they say *my servant."* Thus does extinction overtake the old type of "valiant knights," whom Cervantes in his Don Quixote makes the butt and laughing-stock of light women and chambermaids. This famous satire was written, as every one knows, to laugh out of existence the last vestige of chivalry, already dead to all intents and purposes.

As early as the fifteenth century men had ceased to greet the fair with song. The warlike poetry of Germany, after first passing from the martial to the tender, from the *bardit* (ballad), or war-song pure and simple, to sentimental plaints and the *Frauendienst* or "service of ladies," of a sudden lost all its inspiration. Poetry turns to prose; in fact it would seem as though simultaneously in all countries, even in those where love was most at home, the Sword grew conscious of the faults and artificialities of the fair sex. All symptoms point to the development of such a disillusionment, in presence of which the old-world cult of tender consideration for women disappears. Thus the old primitive sentiment of respect is replaced by a merely artificial affectation of deference, the basis of our modern school of manners.

In the age of the *fabliaux* of *Court Mantel* and *Le*

Comte Ory, the first of a series of many such abominations, of the indecent *Nouvelles* of Louis XI's day,
which represent the Sword as already perverted and
corrupt, there is left no room any more for passionate
enthusiasms, for the chaste love of noble Paladins for
their high-born ladies fair. "My *lady*" was the phrase
of early days, for in those times *mistress* was a word
not in use, a word implying some one a man may do
with as he pleases. Very soon woman, *semper eadem,*
the "eternal feminine," fêted in *other* ways it is true
but still fêted under all changes, wearies of the idolatrous homage of her humble worshippers, and more
and more eager for untrammeled licence, comes down
altogether from off her pedestal. What next? She dons
a mask, exposing at the same time after the German
mode her bosom more freely bared than ever, "the chest
displayed to the very belly," to follow the expression of
a preacher who lived in those happy days.* "The
mask hides all," as Brantôme puts it.

Out of pure gaiety of heart and high spirits did
women prepare and inspire the sensuous, and sensual,
Renaissance, which in imitation of antiquity, devoted
its best energies to the extraction of a quintessence of
pleasurable sensation from physical love. Thus did the
Sword, new born to a new life, penetrated as it were
by the effervescence of a new Springtide, set up a new

---

* Olivier Maillard, Preacher to Louis XI and Confessor
to Charles VIII. He used to cry out in the pulpit, addressing
the ladies of his congregation: "And you, young wenches,
you, women of the court, does this touch *you?*"

cult of Venus consisting in a totally changed worship of
the sex. In it there is no question of the ideal, simply
and solely one of tangible, fleshly beauty cultivated with
every refinement of care, further supplemented by the
additional allurements of all the delights and all the
elaborations of Asiatic luxury.

Women, roused by every stimulus of excitement and
anticipation, and irresistible in their headlong impetu-
osity, carry the Sword along with them on a torrent of
startling changes. Their claims to independence lead
everywhere from South to North to a veritable revolution. Like their contemporary, Columbus, they too
divine a New World; they welcome with a rain of
flowers the dawning of a new era, and crown with
wreaths of violets the conqueror of Italy,* that "soft
land of velvet," where races were run in 1315 in which
the competitors were courtesans.†

In France these fallen divinities had long shown
themselves as patronesses of the licentious tales and
provocative stories which the learned Etienne Pasquier
calls "ladies' divertissement." They had tolerated and
indeed encouraged in all ways in their power, if not

---

* Charles VIII arrives in Italy, and lo! the poor man is
driven half wild with the acclamations of his triumph:
"Ladies crowned him with a garland of violets and greeted
him with kisses as the champion of their honor."—V. de la
COLOMBIERE, Théâtre d'honneur (Theatre of Honor).

† "Castruccio Castracani, to humiliate the Florentines whom
he has driven back into their town, gives under the walls
of Florence a race of courtesans among other amusements."—
VALERY, Curiosités et anecdoctes italiennes. (Italian Curiosities and Anecdotes.)

actually invented, all productions of the kind, adopting
for their own use in the different dialects of love-making certain words of equivocal meaning, and out of
these framing a sort of *argot* or "little language" of
wanton living, a kind of polite *slang*. For this end they
borrow from the most free-spoken writers of the licentious school they have created. At first they utilize the
startlingly outspoken expressions of that scribbling lady,
Christina of Pisa; then as time goes on, their naughty
vocabulary is enriched by "pleasant lubricities" culled
from the literature of their day, beginning with the
Roman de la rose. Next in the series, to supply them
with bad words and smart notions, come Villon's and
Rabelais' full-flavored improprieties, followed up by the
smut of Brantôme, Abbot of *Brotheliande* and first favorite of gallant dames.

The perusal of the old romances and lascivious tales
written specially for their gratification no longer suffic-
ing to fill their leisure time, these wantons, well instructed in letters and "ill-tongued" in speech, will
presently requisition for the merry and gentle diversion
of their elegant idleness the Dialogues of Aretino, or
better still his illustrated works, "then so much in
fashion."

Beroaldus de Verville, Canon of Tours, has the effrontery to entitle his indecent work *Le Moyen de Parvenir,* or "The Right Way with Women." In a word
the tastes of the soldiers and women of the era are such
as to take delight in inventing, applauding and patron-
izing obscenities of every sort, and freely displaying the
grossest licence.

Already French women of high condition had incurred the unfavorable criticism of a contemporary poet.
Under pretence of giving good advice, he recommends
them not to go to church dressed in such a way as to
show some parts of the body naked; not to swear, nor
yet to get drunk; to be rid of the habit of lying and
stealing; to go to the offertory without giggling, and
not to accept presents and jewelry except from a well-
intentioned relative; last of all not to allow men to put
their hands into their gowns too loosely laced. . . .

Judging by these instructive counsels, we are justified
in thinking the gentlewomen of those days, always
only too delighted to wear alluring raiment and "loose
attire," were not much better than "the light women
who get their living by light-lying their bodies."

This dissoluteness of life, noted again and again by
plenty of other writers as well, and serving to entrap
the opposite sex with the bait of novel pleasures, is
everywhere the same, only still more revolting in the
north of Europe than in other parts, for there we find
husbands exhibiting a scandalous complaisance in favor
of the Sword. When a nobleman, says Æneas Silvius,
pays court to a citizen's wife in Germany, the latter's
husband serves the gallant with drink and contrives so
as to leave him alone with the fair one. In the same
prudish land of *Landsknechts* and *Reiters,* while the
lords are away from their castles hunting or fighting,
their wives, meantime drinking at every meal each of
them "four or five quarts of beer," give themselves up
to the coarsest pleasures. A preacher of the Fatherland exclaims on this subject:

"God keep all pious lads from such women and girls who live only to dance a-nights, to the end they may be touched and kissed without shame."

At Lübeck citizens' wives visit places of ill fame at night time, and there conduct themselves after the fashion of the Empress Messalina. In some other towns the professional prostitutes have the right of citizen-ship.* Poggio in 1415 recounted the debaucheries and filthy usages practiced in his day at Baden during the bathing season.†

---

* Dr. Johannes Scherr, *Society and Manners in Germany.*

† If the two sexes mixed and gave themselves up to the most indecent proceedings at the baths of certain German towns, this was still more the case at the famous baths of Baden. "Poggio has given a description of these baths, where during the height of the season merchants and captains came from long distances to take free enjoyment of all kinds of debaucheries, eating and drinking in the bath on floating tables with naked women, and after that dancing with them to the accompaniment of instruments of music and singing."—Dr. Johannes Scherr, *Society and Manners in Germany.*

"Captains, statesmen, merchants and clerks used to come thither from very great distances to enjoy all the refinements of debauchery. In the morning the baths would present an animated scene; those who were not bathing themselves looked on from an elevated gallery at the men and women in the bath, who would be eating and drinking from float-ing tables. Pretty girls would be going about asking them for alms, and displaying alluring charms to tempt their appetite. After the midday rest, drinking went on again as much as the human stomach could endure, till the sound of the instruments gave the signal for dancing."—Poggio, *The Baths of Baden in 1417.*

In earlier times than these, the English monks wrote in 1348: "Heaven hath even now sent the *Black Death* to punish women above all others for their indiscreet interference with men's diversions." Later Matteo Palmieri expressed his indignation at seeing the flower of the ladies of Florence take delight in mimicking the prostitutes in their dress, fashions and ways.* Later again, it is the terrible Plague of Naples which, if we are to believe the general testimony of contemporary accounts, soldiers caught from the Italian women and brought back with them to France,—yet another fatal gift of women to men of the Sword.

Everywhere, at Venice where noble maidens act as prostitutes, at Rome, where the Popes recall and formally reinstate the courtesans whom the ladies of con-

---

* "I have seen," wrote Palmieri about 1450, "I have seen in the city the dress and mien of prostitutes, once looked upon as dishonorable and shameless, presently adopted and imitated at their fêtes and festivals by the flower of the noble Florentine ladies. . . . These ladies would bare their breasts and allow their gowns to fall even right below the bosom."— PALMIERI, *Vita civile* (Life of Cities).—VALERY, *Curiosités et anecdotes italiennes* (Italian Curiosities and Anecdotes).

Holbein represents the German ladies of his century affecting to show the bosom perfectly bare.

"The women of Lombardy, where Galeasso Sforza was in power, had the reputation of being excessively dissolute."

Paulus Jovus, in his book "Famous Men" wrote on this as follows: "The dissoluteness of life was so great at that time, above all among matrons and girls, that any other woman properly regardful of her chastity was held a fool and ill instructed in comparison with the well-mannered courtesans."—CAMERABIUS, *Meditations*.

dition were for supplanting, in Sicily, in Cyprus at Famagousta, where sixty thousand "filles de joie" are said to have plied their trade, in Turkey even, where the odalisques are at that period accused of a form of love "infamous and abominable," in Spain where a native book, *la Célestine,* reveals the mysteries of Castilian immorality, the same habits of debauchery are rife.   There were still to be found in Madrid, in Lope de Vega's time, more than thirty thousand prostitutes.

Under such conditions then, without violent crisis or fierce death agony, did the good old chivalry of heroic days disappear, to be succeeded in the social structure by a new and entirely different epoch, that of gallantry frank and free, with its "outspoken talk," to whose inspiration is due the institution of the Golden Fleece, purely amatory in its reputed origin.*

---

* "Many writers say it was simply because Philip fell in love with a common girl who wore a robe lined with lambskin wool.   Some declare this girl was red-haired and that the prince having gone to see her and having found on her dressing-table a tuft of red hairs, he conceived the idea of ennobling the said tuft of hair by instituting the Order of the Golden Fleece."—Misson, *Nouveau voyage d'Italie* (Second Italian Journey), 1691.

This last version seems to be the true one.

CHAPTER IX

New Ways of Love and Dalliance — Interest in Salacious Art

Women, as just shown, revolted after a time against the idolatrous worship of their humble adorers, and soon completely altered the mode of expressing their respect adopted by the tender sentiment of primitive chivalry. Next in order of consideration comes the period of *gallantry*, an outcome of women's own activity, of the application of their own light-hearted spirits to the new modes of love initiated by them and followed by the Sword.

In the old diction of Castile,—subsequently, however, to the Cid, who was for killing Doña Chimène's doves to show his defiance and threatened to have her skirts cut short above her knees,*—the word *Galanteria*,† a word of Provençal origin and expressing a

---

* Chimène in the old ballads complains how the Cid kills her doves to defy her, and threatens to cut her skirts to an indecent height.

Que me cortara mis faldas
Por vergonzoso lugar.

(That he would cut my skirts to the shameful place.)

Merimee, *Mélanges Historiques et Littéraires* (Historical and Literary Miscellanies), Paris, Lévy, 1867.

† *Galanteria.* Galan, el que anda vestido de gala, y se precia de gentil hombre: y porque los enamorados de ordi-

Provençal idea, is defined thus: "*galanteria,* gallantry, gentle bearing, generosity, good heartedness, enthusiastic tenderness." It sums up in fact everything that is becoming and suitable to the Sword, according to the special tastes and good pleasure of ladies.

Thus employed and thus understood, gallantry marks the decay of disinterested admiration and the continued progress of sentiment towards sensual indulgence. "The last thing to be found in gallantry is love," is La Rochefoucauld's maxim. At a later date Montesquieu gives it as his opinion that the general wish on the part of men to please women was the origin of gallantry, which is not love at all, but rather a kind of delicate flattery, a subtle affectation, a systematic falsity.* Tak-

---

nario andan muy apuestos para aficionar a sus damas, ellas los llaman sus galanes; y communmente decimos: fulano es galan de tal dama. (*Gallantry.* A gallant, one who goes abroad dressed in parade costume, and gives himself out for a gentleman: and inasmuch as lovers as a rule go very elegantly dressed to please their ladies, they call them their gallants and we commonly say: such an one is the gallant of such a lady).—CAROLO BOUILLIO. *Galant,* that is, joyful (laetus), gay in dress and mien.—*Galanteria,* the same as gentility or gentle bearing, and so generous and courteous. To dress gaily, to play the gallant.—COBARRUVIAS, *Dictionary,* under word *Galan.*

* "The bonds that unite us with women originate in the happiness connected with the pleasures of the senses, the charm of loving and being loved, and likewise in the desire of pleasing them, seeing they are very enlightened judges as to a portion of the constituents of personal merit. Of this general desire to please is born gallantry, which is not love, but rather a kind of delicate flattery, a subtle affectation, a systematic falsity in love."—MONTESQUIEU, *De l'es-*

ing these different definitions, dating as they do from different eras, as guides, some idea may be formed of old-world gallantry, as well as the general character-istics of a perfect gallant of the best period. With regard to the epithet *gallant* as applied to women, one which Brantôme in his Treatise on Fair Dames uses of the greatest and most *honorable* ladies of his day,—its inner, esoteric meaning and technical significance may be gathered from a song, a medley of tears and smiles, composed by Marcelle de Castellane on the departure of her lover, the Duc de Guise:

Je m'imagine qu'il prendra
Quelque nouvelle amante,
Mais qu'il fasse ce qu'il voudra,
Je suis la plus galante;
Mon cœur me dit qu'il reviendra,
C'est ce qui me contente.

(I ween he will take some other mistress; but let him do as he will, *I am the most gallant.* My heart tells me he will return, and that thought contents me.)

It would not be easy without wounding delicacy, to give a more ample definition of *gallant* as applied to a lady.

The reign of gallantry in its highest perfection coin-cides pretty exactly in its commencement with that of the fifteenth century, and ends simultaneously with the sixteenth. After 1400 there is no more any question

---

prit des lois, bk. XXVIII, ch. XXII, Des mœurs relatives au combat (Of Morality as related to Fighting and its Customs)

among the princes of Italy or the dukes of Burgundy of love-making in "the old-fashioned coarse way," but only in consonance with rules formulated by the ladies, that is to say, "with all gentleness, and pretty ways and wanton wiles."

This elegant mode, which no doubt in its first essays was still indeterminate, soon acquired its characteristic and definite form "after King Francis the First of France, thinking to pursue love in all gallant gentleness, had to that end established his most excellent court, frequented by such excellent and honorable princesses, great dames and demoiselles, whom he freely availed himself of."* Henceforth, high-born women exert more than ever, thanks to the Sword and the admiration it inspires, a fatal influence over the whole social organ-

---

* "King Francis loved *not wisely but too well*. For being young and free, indifferently did he fondle now one and now another, as in sooth at that time he was not counted gallant who did not go wenching everywhere indiscriminately; whereof he got the pox, which shortened his days. Indeed he died when hardly yet an old man; for he was only fifty-three, which was nothing. Now the king, when he saw himself tormented and afflicted with this disease, was aware that if he did continue these vagabond loves, it would be still worse for him; and so, wise by experience, determined to follow love very gallantly. Wherefore to this end he did establish his excellent court frequented by such excellent and honorable princesses, great dames and demoiselles, whom he did avail himself of only to make sure against unclean diseases and no more to soil his person with the filthiness of other days. Thus did he accommodate and satisfy himself with a love that was no wise foul, but gentle, clean and pure."— BRANTÔME, *Le Grand Roi Henri II* (The Great King Henry II of France).

ism. Their *merry doings,* mimicked by the ranks below
them, their dissolute life, their luxury and extravagant
dress, corrupt the citizen class, then by contagion that
of tradesfolk and artisans.

The wise Montaigne said, speaking of sundry blame-
worthy practices of his day, "Our kings are all powerful in such extreme reforms. . . . The rest of France,
—and he might very well have said the whole of Europe,—takes its cue from the court." "Had it only
been the ladies alone who were dissolute!" observes an
old historian and severe critic of his contemporaries;
"but the worst is the bad example they gave to other
women, who were only too ready to mould themselves
on their costume and affectations, on their dancing and
ways of life. . . ."*

A few words with regards to the prestige and delights in old days of the palaces of kings, those cradles
of gallantry. Think of all that is known of the best
days of elegance and luxurious living, and then picture
how potent an attraction the idea of dwelling with the
king must have exercised over the mind of ladies,
whether of the greater or lesser nobility.

It used to be said in the eighteenth century: "When
far from court, not only is one unhappy, but ridiculous
into the bargain." In the provinces, at the hearth of
castles and manors, where old customs prescribed that
the oldest present sat down to table only after having
offered up a prayer to God by the mouth of a child,
there was mighty little diversion for a woman. Amid

---

* VARILLAS, *History of Henri III.*

this dull domesticity, this life so full of *ennui* and monotony, the day-dreams of young and pretty women, panting for gaiety and gay sights soared away inevitably towards the court. *It* summed up all their longings, *it* possessed all the attraction of the unknown round which their fancy could play. "In such imaginings," Marguerite de Valois used to say, "is no innermost corner (of a woman's being) but is penetrated by some surreptitious, naughty spark of wanton desire." From this same spark, be it noted, spring all the fantastic doings of gallantry.

It is quite sufficient to have read in the *Contes d'Eutrapel* of Noël du Fail, the exact description there given of a country nobleman's residence somewhere about 1530, to form an idea of the dreary monotony that in former days brooded over the mansions of the lords of the soil. These were ever haunted, for the demoiselles of the family and indeed for all ladies of birth who still retained their youth, by an unavowed and unavowable mournfulness like the dreary tortures of a bad dream. This arose from two causes,—there were the languors of April called up by the first fine days and the first appearance of the springtide greenery, the color specially symbolic of Priapus, and there were in the long winter evenings strange thoughts that came unbidden during readings of the *Roman de la Rose* or the *Decameron,* works that figured as a rule side by side on the shelves with the dust-covered Bible.

According to Mme. de Genlis, a woman's first requirement is to be in company—a very venial fault, if only it had not led to so many evil consequences. Provincial *gentlewomen,* who had followed the magnet and taken up their abode at court, no sooner found themselves "in brave attire, decked out with gawds, painted and washed," than their delight was to compromise and corrupt, always from this love of being in company, king, princes and nobles. A score or so of pretty women, smartly dressed, furbelowed and merry-hearted, were thus enough to debauch all the men of the highest rank who formed the court world. Through them it is the word *courtesan* (court-lady in its original acceptation) has got its disgraceful connotation; while everything goes to demonstrate the evil influence they had over sovereigns, whom they invariably tended to set against men of solid merit.

"Small use in France," said de Saulx-Tavannes, "to know battles and assaults, if a man knows not the court and the ladies."

Royal grace and royal favor were disposed of by the court-ladies, who prescribed from that focus of wealth and luxury the fashions, bearing and modes of speech the ambitious nobility of the Sword were to adopt. The government and regulation of high life was in their hands.

Abundant evidence exists to reveal in what ways these lovers of perpetual change, after their open revolt against the apathy of Platonic love, after they had begun to feel the craving for a life of pleasure, set in motion the sensual instincts of gallantry and passion. Everybody knows how towards the end of the era of chivalry, they shook the unwilling sentimentalist out of his lethargy, and constrained their admirers to gratify their desires by the most unseemly favors and familiarities.

In England, Chateaubriand* relates, they had pastry baked in suggestive shapes served at table, while on the South side of the Channel the merry innovators were wont with quips and jest to drink on certain gala days from goblets ornamented with the most abominably indecent figures.

Taking advantage of such encouragements, men of the Sword, their eyes once opened, monstrously abused in a spirit of swaggering emulation the merits they un-doubtedly possessed as lovers. They display, nay! actually exaggerate, by way of additional seduction, both in their sumptuous dress of everyday and in their war harness, a token or phallic emblem of the new shamelessness of life,—that obscene object the *braguette* or cod-piece,† all beribboned in the German mode, and

---

* CHATEAUBRIAND, *Essay on English Literature*, Introduc-tion.

† LOUIS GUYON, bk. LIV, ch. VI of his *Diverses Leçons* (Miscellaneous Information), where he describes the fashions of French costume at that period, says: "The trunk hose were so closely fitted there was no means of making a pocket in them. But instead men used to wear a very large, thick *brayette* or cod-piece, that had two appendages at the two sides, which they fastened on with brooches, one on each side, and in the ample space there was between the said brooches, the shirt and the cod-piece, they used to put their handkerchiefs, an apple, an orange, or other fruits, or their purse; or else if they did not trouble to carry purses, they

serving gallants of 1530 as a comfit-box. *Sic placet Veneri,*—"Such is Love's good pleasure." Thus does tenderness grow entirely material, and women descend to a lower and lower level; while concurrently the no-ble weapon of fighters shrinks into the slender rapier, presently to grow lighter and ever lighter, to be be-dizened with chasings and gold, to become smaller and slenderer in direct ratio with the loss of vigor on the part of the nobles.

Simultaneously with these changes in the sword, there is an increase in the numbers of court ladies—an institution originated and brought to perfection by the same gallant king of France who served as an example in such matters both to his successors and to the other sovereigns of Europe. Then these ladies sell their favors to get the wherewithal to make a brave show and meet the expenses of their sumptuous toilettes, for above all things "it is needful, come what may, to make a figure in kings' palaces." On their side meantime the nobles of the court, with a view to decoying and allur-ing the sex, make the most extravagant display in dress, grown *très gorgias,* as the phrase went at the Louvre, even before the days when Catherine de Médici traf-ficked there for political ends in the charms and naugh-

---

would put their money in a slit they made on the outside, near the head or point of the aforesaid cod-piece. And it was considered polite, when at table, to offer fruits that had been kept some time in this cod-piece, as to the present day some men offer fruits from their pocket."

"How much the cod-piece is chief part in the harness among fighting folk."—RABELAIS, *Pantagruel,* ch. VIII.

tiness of her maids of honor. To gratify a court-lady—
Mlle. de Montmorency—Henry IV, at the age of fifty-
three tilted at the ring, wearing a perfumed lace collar
and sleeves of China satin.

The preceding considerations will suffice to show
how the official character, so to speak, assumed by love
among men of the Sword depended absolutely on the
caprice of women, always the arbiters of masculine
fashion. It now behooves us to hark back once more
in the course of our analysis, to pick up again the
broken chronological thread.

The fifteenth century, then, was the period of all
others when gallantry most flourished amid a brilliant
confusion of glittering gold and bronze, velvet and
flashing steel, amid art and songs and merry dances,
amid fêtes and masquerades, where lips were but too
ready to meet and kisses readily exchanged. Gallantry
was the most marked and distinctive expression of the
represented on its intellectual and religious side by the
irresistible collective activity of women and the Sword,
an activity that impressed on the men of those days an
extraordinary vivacity and mobility of mind. War in
Southern Europe, as for instance at the date of the
Peloponnesian War, declared at Aspasia's bidding, has
invariably been accompanied by a stirring of the soul
tending in the highest degree to the furtherance of the
arts. Later again, in Italy, the licence arrogated by the
Sword and still more that of ladies and of courtesans,
"who in Lombardy wear gowns of cloth of gold and
look like fairies," all tend to stimulate the merely car-

nal worship of women. This worship, as we know, exasperated the sour morality of contemporaries, and is
represented on its intellectual and religious side by the
gloomy and violent Savonarola, that sworn foe of false
hair and love of dress.

Loving all forms of plastic and painted representa-
tion everywhere—in palaces and even in the baths of
Pope Julius II* in the Vatican, mythology (that had
re-appeared once more in Italy under Charlemagne)
exhausts itself anew in lascivious images.

Artists imbued with the ruffling spirit of their day,
like Leonello Spada, Benvenuto Cellini, or Caravag-

---

* The Baths of Julius II are on the third story of the
Vatican and are well-nigh forgotten nowadays. This part of
the building is bordered externally towards the court-yard
by a hanging gallery formed of planks. The way to them
is by broad staircases, the inclination of these being so
gentle as to allow mules to bring the water up into the
garrets of the palace.

The room where his Holiness used to come to bathe is
at most nine or ten feet long. It formed, a few years since,
part of the lodgings of a Papal Chamberlain, and it was
very difficult to gain admittance.

Lighted by a single arched window with gilded mouldings
round it, the apartment is symmetrically decorated with
priceless paintings by Rafael, on a reddish ground. The
subjects represent scenes of great licentiousness: satyrs,
women and fauns, Cupid teasing Venus, and in the fore-
ground Apollo caressing a complaisant nymph. These paintings, which are engraved in the works of the artist, are
in the main still in very good preservation. The three side
walls, without windows, each show a small niche or recess
in which no doubt were put the perfumes and vases of
scented waters.

gio, take a heartfelt delight and pride in exalting in
their works, copied after the antique, the graceful
beauty of the sex, so unfairly depreciated in the artistic
productions of the Middle Ages, when Germany went
so far as to make even her *Liebfrau,* her "dear Virgin,"
unprepossessing. In this new era of form and beauty,
the Madonna of the South, *Maria formosa,* Mary most
beautiful, who tends to get younger and ever younger
as represented in art, loses her stiff, rigid look, grows
graceful, even a trifle affected, and before long appears
décolleté, while the Magdalen, the Madelon of later
days, whence the Madelonettes, pushes yet further a
naturalness that is on the high road to indecency.

Titian, Giorgione and other favored artists chosen
to serve the "gilded youth of the Sword," portray absolutely naked, or to use the technical phrase, "paint in
the nude," high-bred courtesans of beauteous shape
and red-gold hair, and even some *honorable ladies*
under the same conditions. Bandello, Bishop of Agen,
relates how a young nobleman of Vicenza lost his wife
outright at this game.*

All these sensuous productions of the brush, exalting
the grace and elegance of the nude female form, were
nothing more nor less than so many suggestive adver-
tisements to the advantage of the fair sex. So alluring
a state of affairs naturally stirred all sensual desires to
fever heat, and determined that effervescence of gallantry which spread throughout Europe from South to

---

* BANDELLO, *Hist. Traigiques* (Tragic Histories), vol. II,
No. XXXIV, p. 637 (French transl. by Chapuy).

North, and was so coarsely mimicked in lands beyond the Rhine.

German women were even more ready than in the preceding century, in certain towns of the Fatherland, to display their charms scarcely veiled at all under transparent muslins, while ladies of title no less than citizens' wives used without a blush to bathe at the public baths, promiscuously and perfectly nude, along with "all sorts and conditions of men."*

In Flanders, in Touraine, the "fairest and most demure" of maidens, even daughters of noble houses, stirred by such examples—modesty we must remember, according to Seneca's opinion, is not really of the feminine gender at all—would sometimes figure undraped and as decorative accessories in the ceremonials attending triumphs of the Sword or in the gorgeous entertainments held under its auspices. It was so at Antwerp in 1520 on occasion of the visit of Charles the Fifth,† later again at the entry of Henry II of France into Blois,‡ or once again in 1577

---

* DR. JOHANNES SCHERR, Society and Manners in Germany.

With regard to the physical defects of German women in the fifteenth century, see a drawing by Albert Dürer (1496) preserved in the Kunsthalle of Bremen.

† At Antwerp, for the triumphal entry of the king, "the gates were adorned with allegorical representations, young girls almost naked; I have rarely seen such beautiful women." —ALBERT DURER, Journey in the Low Countries, 1520-21. These young maidens, who had on only a transparent gauze, were the most beautiful girls in Antwerp.

‡ HENRI ESTIENNE, Apology for Herodotus.

at the royal banquet of Plessis-lez-Tours, where "half-naked and with hair flowing loose, like brides," the most beautiful of the court-ladies waited at table.*

No external authority would have ventured to forbid or even interfere with these lascivious diversions, which recall some festival of Anoumati, the Hindoo goddess of sexual licence. Such displays, where woman loved to expose all the entrancing beauties of her nature, were far too well protected by the brutalized Sword; and the most finished wantons could safely, braving the looks of the startled public and the reprimands of preachers, themselves corrupt, show off their beauty as much and as audaciously as they pleased. Thus was established under the auspices of high-born ladies a new deification of woman as an instrument of carnal love, under cover of the motto, "Honi soit qui mal y pense."†

---

* Pierre l'Estoile, *Journal*—year 1577.

Other banquets of the same kind took place about this time at Chenonceau. The general arrangements and scenery, which were highly indecent, were under the superintendence of the Queen Mother.

Women, whatever they may *say* about their modesty, always love in their fashions to expose their charms as much as possible.

† "Motto of the Order of the Garter, created in 1350 by Edward III, of England, in honor of a garter of the Countess of Salisbury, which she had dropped while dancing and which the king had picked up. Some authorities throw doubt on the story."—Antoine Furetiere, *Dictionary*, under word Jarretière (Garter).

CHAPTER X

Spread of Gallantry Establishes Indecent Language — Sapphism and Naughty Tales

Fashion is almost invariably propagated from South to North, and the spread of gallantry forms no exception to the rule; the hankering for carnal pleasure beginning in Southern lands, flooded all parts of Europe. From Spain, with its Arab and Moorish strains, it soon invaded France, where the indigenous frivolity of the French temperament melted into and made one with it, like Arethusa losing herself in the bosom of Alpheus. Simultaneously it made its appearance in Italy, and somewhat later in Hungary, where not a few Eastern habits were acclimatized; while among our neighbors of the North it was virtually unrecognizable under the tasteless travesty it there showed itself.

This new type of love, with an ever growing audacity, soon ventured on the coarsest phraseology. These new sensual modes copied from antiquity, to meet women's wishes and satisfy the unanimous cravings of the five senses, Boccaccio, Sacchetti, Poggio, Giraldi, Centhio, Bandello, Rabelais, Falengo, Brantôme— whose diction is that of the *honorable* ladies of his period—and many another indiscreet, prying teller of naughty tales, are far and away more instructive

than formal history, which is either pedantic by convention or else dumb by constraint. Not that *dumb*
is precisely the right word, seeing that by Marmontel's
calculation, it would require eight hundred years, and
fourteen hours' work a day all the year round, to read
all the volumes of history printed up to 1660 only.

In investigations of every kind details should be
studied first, in order at a subsequent stage to elaborate the series of special observations made into a
general survey of the subject. This is the only way to
get good results. The light literature of manners,
nouvelles, memoirs and the like, is what provides by its
indiscretions by far the most definite body of information available under the present head. Whether these
frank revelations are found in the *Decameron*, the
Heptameron or the *Astraea;* whether they are described
in the preparations for a tourney or recounting the
delicate adventures of anonymous heroes; it is there
we must seek material for scrutinizing the old-world
life of gallantry, there exhibited unreservedly in the
plain garb of truth, vices and deformities laid bare
no less than good points and attractive features.*

---

* Bandello has given (*Nouvelles*, vol. IV, 4th part, no.
26) a description of the bed-chamber of a *gentildonna* of his
time. Elegance of furniture counted for a great deal in
the sixteenth century in matters of gallantry.

"A very handsome young widow, taking advantage of
carnival time," he relates, "induces her foster-father to
invite a handsome gentleman, whom she has remarked and
with whom she has fallen in love, to visit her. The young
man is received by the lady in her palace, magnificent with

If the inner character of a people can be approxi-
mately gauged by their popular songs, or even simply
by their demeanor, their quips and cranks, at moments
of festivity, *a fortiori* may an opinion be formed of
their life and habits from the authentic writings of
their story-tellers.

From the thirteenth century downwards, this literature of indiscretion divulges the inmost details of
private life. Thanks to its delightful, outspoken tattle,
and above all among the people of the South, (for

---

its priceless tapestries and carpets of Alexandria. He is
introduced into the low-ceilinged apartment serving as her
bed-chamber; the bed is adorned with curtains of marvelously
rich workmanship and two fair pillows of purple silk admi-
rably embroidered with gold thread and delicately perfumed.

"On a little table in a silver candlestick burns a *torchetto,*
a wax light of the whitest wax; on the same table, which
is covered with a silken cloth woven in divers colors and
embroidered with silk and gold intermingled after the fashion of Alexandria, are ranged in order combs of ivory and
ebony for combing the beard and hair, elegant caps, dressing-
robes for throwing round the shoulders when dressing the
hair, and dainty towels of the finest linen. In lieu of tapestry
the room was hung with cloth of gold with velvet panels.
In each panel were coats of arms belonging to the family
of the late husband, and that of the widow, hers being hid
under needlework hangings that they might remain unknown.
In charming vases of majolica had been provided the most
exquisite confections and the precious wines of Montebrian-
tino.

". . . Before seeing the gentleman to bed, the bed is
warmed by means of a *scaldaletto* (warming-pan) of silver;
and finally, after having extinguished fire and candles, the
lady who came with face concealed, gets into bed, putting
her mask for the night, till dawn break, behind the pillow."

indeed the North possesses in the way of *Nouvelles* hardly anything besides its *Gesammtabentheuer,* or "Century of German Tales") we are familiar enough with the good and evil fortunes of the Sword, with the extravagances of dress of the men who had their very horses scented,* to go prancing under the win- dows of their fair and fickle mistresses.† This class of

---

* The following is a description of the gala dress of an Italian exquisite of about 1560:

"He was of a handsome person and dressed with great richness; he changed his costume very often, finding all day long new fashions of embroidery, open lace-work and other gawds. His velvet caps bore now one medal, now another; I say nothing on the chapter of chains, rings, and bracelets. The mounts he rode through the town, whether mule or jennet, Turk or hackney, were as clean as a new pin. The beast he was to ride on was, under its rich trappings, studded with hammered gold, always scented from head to foot, in such wise that the perfume of the com- pounds of musk, civet, amber and other precious essences could be smelt all along the street. Romano, their perfumer, used to say publicly that Messer Simpliciano brought him more gain in a week than any twenty other young noblemen of Milan afforded him in a whole year, always excepting however his Lordship Ambrogio Visconti, who was exceed- ingly lavish in his expenditure on perfumes.

"Simpliciano might vie with the Portuguese dandy who every ten paces, whether he was on foot or on horseback, had his boots cleaned by an attendant."—BANDELLO, *Nou- velles,* 2nd part, no. 47.

† "Meantime a number of French gentlemen, lords and knights, never left off coming and going in this street, gazing at the ladies and making their horses curvet and prance. The horses were excellent, but badly ridden. The greater part of these horsemen were armed, and they rode

literature, and this only, depicts for us the finical affections of the king's favorites, who "painted, combed, rainbow-hued, scented with aromatic powder, perfumed the streets, public places and houses they frequented"* . . . "accoutred with a silken vest without sleeves, their doublet of fine grenadine cloth edged with green and slashed at the elbows, close-fitting cap of red and hat on top of it, from which hangs a gay bouquet most daintily arranged."† Such were the gallants in Italy, who enjoyed nocturnal assignations in low-browed vaulted halls where some fair *gentildonna* awaited them, intoxicated with love and longing and wearing at her bosom the anemone, Venus' flower, the flower of sighs, or perhaps a sprig of marjoram; in Spain, the *embevecidos* (men drunk with love), who drank the wind their mistresses had breathed,‡ who

---

down such persons as were in their road."—Letter of Castiglione addressed from Milan, October 8, 1499, to Messer Jacopo Boschetto de Gonzague, his brother-in-law, in J. DUMESNIL, *Histoire des amateurs italiens.*

* 'Likewise they were used to bear on their accoutrements many powders, and on their clothes, their muffs, their handkerchiefs and collars, such things as musk and Cyprus essence, perfumes and many sachets of aromatic powders, Cyprus powder, as well as civet."—GRATIEN DU PONT, Sieur de DRUSAC, *Des controverses des sexes masculin et féminin* (Controversies of the Two Sexes, Male and Female), Paris, 1540.

† NOEL DU FAIL, *Contes et Discours d'Eutrapel* (Tales and Discourses of Eutrapel).

‡ *Beber los vientos por ella* (to drink the winds for her) was a love phrase in Spain, meaning to be madly in love, in other words, to breathe the same air as the loved object,

loved *hablar à la reja* (love-talk at the barred window),
moonlight serenades and duels, sinister adventures with
jealous husbands, skirmishes with street braggarts and
highway bandits and bravos; they were the stout-
hearted soldiers who followed love and war with equal
ardor, whose delight was in brawls with the watch
and wrangles with the "Captain of the Night," meet-
ings of gallantry in church, at sermon, in the public
walks, now with ladies of the world, now with nuns
painted and masked.*

Such profligacy, though even yet showing traces
of the old manliness in manner and carriage, is all
but universal; and nowhere more than at the court
of France, where in 1560 the Duc d'Este expressed his
wonder to find a maid, and where the court-ladies hid
the result of their lapses from virtue by means of

---

to desire her ardently.—CERVANTES, *Romances.*

The name *Embevecidos*, that is to say "drunk with love,"
was given to men who were so taken up with their passion
and the delight of being by their mistress' side that they
showed themselves incapable of attending to anything else;
and "so it was permitted them to omit uncovering as to a
man who has lost his wits." MME. D'AULNOY, *Relation du
Voyage d'Espagne* (Account of her Spanish Journey), vol. III.

* "On Wednesday, December 8th (1593), Commolet
preached a sermon against the nuns, declaring that men of
birth walked with the same every day in Paris, so that in
very truth nothing was to be seen but gentlemen and nuns
arm in arm, the said nuns wearing under their veil the
regular dress and ornaments of courtesans, painted, powdered,
masked and foul-mouthed. The aforesaid Commolet be-
labored them right well."—P. DE L'ESTOILE, *Journal*, Dec.,
1593.

farthingales invented for that very end, had gallantry attained a more refined and perfect sensuality. Yet with all its hard recklessness, at times it still betrays a refractory instinct making in spite of all for the old-fashioned respect and sentimental tenderness towards women, an instinct the enterprising fair ones of the day cannot abide. It is a sort of survival, a hereditary *sport,* a reminiscence of the old *prudish* fashions long since abandoned. The Sword indeed, it should be observed, had all along wished to respect women, a thing not always easy to do, and after a while all but impossible, when women left off respecting themselves.

After having been in the first instance, once more to repeat the statement, treated as goddesses on earth by the Swordsmen of heroic and chivalrous ages, women once and for all chose gallantry as better representing their tastes. They would fain, by publicly displaying an intentional absence of dignity, be rid of the tiresome cult of worship and respect that dogged their steps and hemmed them in. They laugh undisguisedly at desperate lovers, "givers of bouquets and silly flowers," lovers who "waxing melancholy, full of protestations and lunatic proceedings generally, would indulge in early morning serenades and appear masked to offer them the holy water at Church." They look upon marks of respect now as mere affectation, and claim the right to change lovers when and how they please. Such are the laws of the women's code.

Nevertheless, just as in the days of sentiment and of

fanatical devotion to ladies, when men staked "heart
and body and soul" on love, women still exact from
mere motives of vanity, even under the new régime
of gallantry, some tokens of passionate attachment.
To this end they make capital out of the affected non-
sense of the romances. Lanoue points out a great
danger threatening the nobility of France in the habit-
ual perusal of the romances of Amadis of Gaul, "which
by their conceits are working its ruin." Finally, as
could not but happen, the less simple-minded swains
end by protesting against absurd follies such as these:
Salignac wishes to poison himself, and indeed supposes
himself to do so, for the bold and dissolute Marguerite de Valois, who laughs at him for his pains;*
another gentleman, a man of birth of Auvergne, in
deference to a caprice of Mlle. de Cornon jumps into
the Allier booted and sword at side. A Mons. de
Genlis does the same in the Seine, to fish out the
handkerchief of a wanton, who only makes fun of
him.† Candale for love's sake turns Protestant—no
small thing to do in those days; while Bussy d'Amboise
according to Tallemant des Réaux, or according to
Brantôme, Mons. de Lorges, on the precedent of an
old legend, jumps into a lion's den to recover the glove
a court lady or maid of honor has thrown down to
test his devotion. Such are some of the acts of sense-
less recklessness performed at this period out of mere

---

* TALLEMANT DES REAUX, *Historiettes;* Queen Marguerite,
vol. I.
† TALLEMANT DES REAUX, *Historiettes,* vol. V.

gallantry or in an access of *broken-hearted* love, to use the English phrase.

"In love and war, for one pleasure a thousand pains," says an old French proverb. Say, rather, a thousand follies! These continued still in fashion in the days of the cavaliers. Tallemant des Réaux relates that the Comte de Grandpré would drink his mistress' health out of a loaded and cocked pistol, with his finger on the trigger, and how another of these "love's mad-men," used to swallow, and narrowly escaped suffoca-tion in the process, the ribbons their ladies had given them.

From Cleopatra's time, whose amusement was to make Marc Antony angle for salted fish, love-sick swains have been cajoled into many a foolish and compromising eccentricity. Surviving till well into the seventeenth century, they still occasionally retain a smack of the "noble paladin and courteous knight" of an earlier day; while in other cases again they present, side by side with true feelings of honor, the strangest contrast of coarseness and brutality. Thus the Duc de Bellegarde,* though notoriously kept by the wife of a president of Council, continued, in spite of his equivocal, or rather unequivocal, position, one of the last sticklers for these exaggerations of chivalrous devotion. Starting on a campaign, he fell on his knees

---

* "Bellegarde was a General Officer and Commander of Saint-Louis; he had been a very well-made man and very *gallant,* and had long been kept by the wife of one of the first magistrates of the Parliament."—SAINT-SIMON, *Memoirs.*

before Anne of Austria, with whom he professed himself in love—a successor to Mazarin and the Duke of
Buckingham—and begged her to touch the hilt of his
rapier.

Nevertheless, in spite of these last flickers of the old
sentimental infatuation, the Sword is now to proclaim
outright its scorn and contempt for women. In face of
constantly recurring scandals, the bourgeoisie, growing independent as it grows in self-importance, as well
as the commonalty, become altogether hostile to the
nobility of both sexes, the prestige and dignity of the
whole class diminishing ever more and more in their
eyes.

Sin after sin of self-indulgence is committed in the
face of day, and the continual progress of popular ill-
will can be readily followed: revolt against the higher
classes is ever organizing, strengthening and spreading
in France from the date of the first rising of the
"League" and its accompanying disorders. In all places
and at all times since, the movement has reappeared
again and again, at once overweening in its consequence, self-seeking in its ends, and stupid in its means.

In proportion as fresh grievances revive the excitement does it assume a character more and more aggres-
sive, always finding a convenient pretext in the public
wrongs. Now, indeed, there appears among the first
fruits of the newly invented printing press, taking the
place of the old-fashioned romances of chivalry and
tales of martial adventure—works of imagination in the
main inspired by female influence—a new class of

literature, definitely hostile to women, and in which a spirit of active revolt against their predominance is manifested, while simultaneously the popular enmity grows more marked than ever and the general ill-esteem in which they are held more pronounced.

In a metrical tale (Fabliau) of the fourteenth century* occurs a menace addressed to the frail beauties of the day who have already fallen into discredit: "This day shall be known the faith you keep with those good knights that bear so many toils and troubles for your sake." In the same widely read work we learn, amongst other mysterious particulars, how the fine ladies of olden times made use of perfumed baths, into which, by a refinement of curious sensuality, or of cleanliness possibly, they were wont to admit new lovers.

Still more complete are other revelations of the printing-press, an invention now brought to full perfection: it shows us the poet who continued and completed the *Roman de la Rose* openly appeasing with yet another insult the sex he had grossly and coarsely offended. It tells us what disease Queen Claude died of, and how determined the famous Admiral de Bonnivet was to sieze by force the "Marguerite of Marguerites," the pearl of pearls, the enticing sister of his sovereign, whose private schemes he thus ran the risk of thwarting.

All this information is further supplemented by

---

* Fabliau of *Court Mantel*.

the literary confidences of a number of female writers, who commit high treason, as it were, against
themselves and their sisters, and contravene the sacred
esprit de corps of their sex. For two hundred years
past these have been revealing the most intimate of
their naughty instincts. This remark we felt bound to
make, incidentally, at this point.

Both in Italy and France it is, as already insisted
on in a previous page, the minor poets and the writers of the lighter literature of the day, beginning with
the tales of Boccaccio and the *Contes* of the Queen of
Navarre, who have best delineated the manners of their
age. We are but ill acquainted with the old-world
life and ways of such peoples as did not possess this
type of literature to reveal their secrets to us.

Thanks to the indiscretions of the writers of *Nouvelles* and anecdotes, it is easy to see how, towards
the end of the sixteenth century, martial love, changing once again in its outward forms of manifestation,
enters so to speak on a moulting season, and presently
takes on an entirely novel aspect.

"The love intrigues of the court, which had never
been in abeyance since the reign of François I, who
had drawn the high-born ladies of France to his court
and lodged them there, when Henri III mounted the
throne, fell into quite intolerable excesses," writes
Varillas.* "The queen of this debauch of gallantry

---

* VARILLAS, *History of Henri III of France* (1589), vol.
VI, xii.

was," he adds, "Mme. de Sauves,* wife of a Secretary
of State." Here we find displayed to the light of day,
for the information of modern times, the spectacle of
the daughter of a noble house turning courtesan, and
a hundred times more lascivious.

"The French ladies of these days welcomed only
offers of service from which they could derive satisfaction for their vanity, while for the main part they
were far from difficult in granting their favors, discretion, of course, always assured," is the assertion of the
same Varillas, whom we have just seen arraigning
Mme. de Sauves.

While self-interest and pleasure thus follow their
bent, the high-born lady, the pride of fairest womanhood, more and more loses her sense of self-respect
—an indisputable sign of social degeneracy. Sap-
phic practices are widely followed, while the author-
ess of the *Ruelle mal assortie* (Ill-mated Bed-fellows),†
the new Queen of Navarre, who was already debauched at the age of eleven, lavishes her favors on a
score or more "of rufflers, foppish young lords and
others."

Everything at this period points to a marked dimi-

---

* MME. DE SAUVES (Charlotte de Beaune-Samblançay),
born about 1551.

† MARGUERITE DE VALOIS, *La ruelle mal assortie, ou Entre-
tiens amoureux d'une dame éloquente avec un cavalier gascon.*
(Ill-mated Bed-fellows, or Amorous Conversations between
an Eloquent Lady and a Cavalier of Gascony), Paris, 1644.

The *Divorce satyrique* gives the names of 23 chief lovers
of Queen Margot.

nution, in the gentlemen and fighter, of his old bodily vigor, for the weight of his arms now makes him consumptive. Without a doubt he is just as brave as were his ancestors, but conscious of being no longer robust enough to face either the vices or the mêlées and tourneys of yore, he adopts as most suitable to his flaccid muscles, the new ways of killing offered him by the use of artillery and firearms generally, now brought to a condition of full efficiency.

Military spirit is lost in the strangest confusion of conflicting notions, for henceforward the gentleman is bound to reckon with *arms of long range*, the use of which he had always hitherto despised as unworthy of him.

CHAPTER XI

Transition from Age of Gallantry to Age of Cavaliers — Minions, Flagellants and Extravagant Luxuries

Towards the end of the sixteenth century, the effects resulting from the interaction of Sword and Sex are once again manifested under fresh aspects. This time they mark the epoch of transition connecting the period of gallantry and the gallants with that of the cavaliers.

Already the young nobility of the Sword, as shown above, is sadly enfeebled by debauchery. The exhausted gallant, "the veteran servant of Venus," is good for hardly anything now but to make a *fop* or a minion: and so these minions, these courtiers turned courte-sans,* refuse to put on armor any more, the weight of which they no longer possess the strength to support.

Under Henri III of France, exquisites carried this effeminacy so far as to have their sword carried by a lackey, on occasion accompanied by bravos in their pay.† Nothing is too bad for these emasculated

---

* "All scented with musk and civet. These folk call themselves courtiers, well-dressed and polished; but by their ways and habits if you will measure them with the eye of reason, you will say they were not men, but harlots."— Theophile Folengo.

† In the sixteenth and seventeenth centuries, people of

creatures, "lurching from one foot to the other, with a half turn of the body, and with heads elaborately curled." They welcome shame as a road to fortune, making themselves all the while ludicrous with their extravagance of dress.

After sacrificing honor to ambition, these *decadents,* these "bedizened swaggerers," marry ladies of the court, the refuse of the king's amours.

About the year 1580, to divert the maids of honor and other fair ladies of the Louvre, the court was in the habit of going abroad with them *masked,* and after committing various follies among the humbler *bourgeoisie,* finally making them join the processions of the Flagellants, where the best made dames figured naked, L'Estoile supplies details of the most indecent nature. Seeing such licence and such shameless self-exposure,* the commonalty show signs of a sour, silent

---

condition had themselves attended by bravos in their pay and armed lackeys. . . . "And that is why you see yonder lackey with all that grand accoutrement and that dagger with guarded hilt."—AGRIPPA D'AUBIGNE, *Les Aventures du baron de Fœneste* (The Adventures of the Baron of Fœneste).

"And nowadays we often see men of a low extraction despise the nobility and play the hero, because they are surrounded by a great number of insolent, ill-conditioned lackeys, who carry long *swords,* and very often pocket-pistols, to guard their master, who, proud and haughty to have such an armed cohort at his side, swaggers and looks askance at the most virtuous and noblest gentlemen who may not possess the means to indulge in such expense."—V. DE LA COLOMBIERE, *Le Vray Théâtre d'honneur et de chevalerie* (The True Theatre of Honor and Knighthood).

* The processions of the *battus* (flogged) were led by the

indignation against the noble classes. They give themselves to every sort of vile habit, and wearying of
commonplace bestiality, "they debauch pages of the
court." "The names of minions," L'Estoile states, "be-
gins at this date to be bandied about on the lips of the
populace, to whom they were intensely odious, as well
for their mocking, insolent ways as for their foolish
ornaments and womanish, immodest dress. . . ."

A careful examination will discover in these novel
fashions of living the persistent influence of "the eternal feminine," to use Goethe's expression, women from
Eve downwards having always notoriously represented
the love of dainty feeding.

Everywhere, towards the end of the age of gallantry,
and this first of all in Italy, later in France also, the

---

king himself at the head of all his court. To adopt Brantôme's expression, "there were ladies, beautiful and pleasant
in converse, well accomplished and all palpitating to set
the world on fire."

"God be thanked!" we read in a document of the time
quoted by Dulaure (History of Paris), "there are such and
such parishes where as many as five or six hundred persons are to be seen taking part in these processions all naked."
On the 14th of February in the same year (1589), other
processions of the sort took place, notably in the parish of
Saint-Nicolas-des-Champs, in which were more than a thousand persons in a state of absolute nudity. All this went
well with the vices of the time.

"In these days (April, 1589), to rob a man's neighbor, to
murder his nearest relatives, to plunder altars, to desecrate
churches, to violate wives and maids, to hold every living
soul to ransom, is the regular business of a Leaguer."—
PIERRE DE L'ESTOILE, *Journal*.

young nobility of the Sword gets more and more
effeminate and corrupt. Everywhere, through women's
fault, the habits of ancient Sodom are found, as practiced in the Isle of the Hermaphrodites, the rites and
mysteries of which have been recorded by Cardinal
du Perron. In this isle the *minions* carry rapiers
and perfumed blades.* Forty of these puny blades
were needed, at the States General of Blois, to dare
the murder of the Duc de Guise, a single man coming
out alone and enervated from a night passed with one
of the fairest of the court ladies—so writes Miron.†

The ruffling swordsmen of the period, the dissolute
exquisities of those swaggering days, little accustomed
as they were in war to the action of explosives, found
themselves completely out of their bearings in face of
the arquebus-fire of the foot-men.

Thus the fighting nobility, in presence of the mere
caprices of fortune annihilating in action skill and
strength alike, lost to some degree its old feeling of
native pre-eminence in battle. Conscious of their
progressive enfeeblement by hereditary taint, while
simultaneously women with never-flagging activity and
enterprise co-operated in the process with all the

---

* *Description de l'isle Hermaphrodites nouvellement décou-
verte.* (Description of the Isle of the Hermaphrodites lately
discovered)—CARDINAL DU PERRON—or ARTUS THOMAS.

† The lady in question was Mme. de Marmoutier (Charlotte de Beaune)—*Relation de la mort du duc de Guise par
le sieur Miron, médecin du Roy Henri III* (Account of the
Death of the Duc de Guise, by the Sieur Miron, physician
to King Henri III).

resources of their sexual charm, they are after 1560 given up wholly and entirely to boasting and quarrel-ing, growing ever more quick to take offence and fond of the duel. They cultivate an exaggerated sensi-tiveness to insult, while fencing becomes more and more complicated and the point of honor more refined than ever. This is the heydey of fencing schools and "pretty bits of bravado." Men fight now in pairs, in fours or even larger bands, like the gladiators of antiquity. In this way, in France alone, within the space of eighteen years, four thousand gentlemen* got themselves killed.

---

* President HENAULT, in his *Abrégé de l'Histoire de France* (Abridgment of the History of France), says that the express prohibition of dueling by Henri II, so far from making these more rare, had made them commoner than before.

"In March, 1607, the king (Henri IV) was advised that since his Majesty's accession to the throne it was calculated that four thousand gentlemen of birth had been killed in these wretched duels, which for a period of eighteen years, gives very nearly two hundred and twenty a year."—L'ES-TOILE, *Journal du règne de Henri IV* (Journal of the Reign of Henri IV).

"In this same month of August (1607) there took place between Poitou and Anjou a duel between thirty gentlemen of birth, the result being that twenty-five were left dead on the field, while the five wounded were in hardly better case. The chiefs of the quarrel were the Sieur de Brézé and the Sieur de Saint-Gemme. The Maréchal de Brissac went to the king and informed him of the facts, who, however, took no action in the matter."—PIERRE DE L'ESTOILE, *Journal.*

These duels in bands recall very ancient customs. In Italy, at Ravenna, at Orvieto, at Sienna, there were held in the Middle Ages combats of gladiators; on certain fixed

With the almost universal adoption of the dagger
as a subsidiary weapon along with the sword, as the
new rules of fencing prescribe,* the habits of swordsmen undergo yet another modification in Europe.
Italian fashions, sullied with sundry faults of their own,
now combine French braggadocio in "unlimited and
extravagant swagger." Simultaneously the bold ways
of wooing which had replaced the long, slow methods
of an earlier school of love-making, now long since dis-
credited, degenerate into sheer insolence and lubricity.

From the days when Queen Margot wore a wig
made of the golden hair of her servants and pages,
and all round her hoop carried the hearts of her
lovers *dead and gone;*† in the days when the saying
"Tout va comme Margot, et Margot comme tout,"

---

days two troops of armed citizens would fight and kill each
other to amuse the crowd.

"In 1346 Petrarch expresses his indignation at seeing the
revival at Naples of the butcheries of the Coliseum."—
VALERY, *Curiosités et Anecdotes italiennes* (Italian Curiosities
and Anecdotes).

* The use of the dagger as seconding the sword in fencing
and dueling, according to the Italian method, dates only from
the sixteenth century. From 1560 to about 1640 this practice
became, to speak generally, universal in Europe. "Double
arms" was the term applied to the sword and dagger, both
being mounted with equally elaborate workmanship. Hence
the common phrase of refusal. A man would say, to
excuse himself for not giving something asked for, "I have
the dagger as well"—implying, I won't give it up, any more
than I will my sword.

† "Queen Margot used to wear a great hoop having little
pockets all around, in each one of which she put a box

great ladies used to talk *Phœbus* (artificial bombastic court dialect),* and even made their male companions do the same. In the same way they taught their cavaliers at the court of the Louvre to lightly trifle with love.

Curtailing its duration, they gave wings, so to speak, to love, so that after 1569, affairs of the sort are conducted at full speed from day to day, mere matters of opportunity and the fancy of the moment. Their ephemeral intrigues are carried through at racing pace; kiss follows quick on kiss, while every thought for the future is excluded by mutual consent from these rapid, frivolous, forced combinations—which are not without a charm, such is the indescribable fascination women command. In such times of never-ending struggle and fighting, the uncertainty of the morrow gives no time for delay; to use an expression of Plutarch's, "it is war in the midst of pleasure, and pleasure snatched in the midst of war."

---

containing the heart of one of her lovers dead and gone; for she was careful, as each of them died, to have the heart embalmed. This hoop was hung up every night on a hook secured by a padlock, behind the head of her bed."— TALLEMANT DES REAUX, *Historiettes;* no. 15. Queen Marguerite, vol. I.

* Compare in England the "Euphuism"—so named from the chief character in John Lyly's two books, *Euphues, the Anatomy of Wit* and *Euphues and his England* (1573 and 1580),—current at the courts of Elizabeth and James I. See Sir Walter Scott's Monastery,—Sir Piercie Shafton; also for extravagance in dress of the time, Note on Chapter X of same novel. (Transl.)

Love is never named now—only love-affairs: and like the lark at dawn, these are swift to be away and on the wing with a trill of song.

Women at this epoch—indeed ever since the Reformation times—"sin, pray, confess, and—begin again." This was the age that invented the suggestive epithet of *maitresse volante* (flying mistress), a phrase well expressing an easiness of morals at once very frank and very French.

Life in those days was spent amid all the intoxication, all the lavish expenditure of force, of an existence stirred to feverish activity by the most potent stimulants. It was a hard life! Women bore up sturdily; but not a few gallants, caught between two fires, like the escutcheon of Naples between its two sirens, *blasé*, harassed—more than ever war harassed and fatigued them—took the monk's frock in sheer lassitude and satiety. Hence the old Spanish proverb, which we may translate, "when the devil had had his fill, the devil a monk would be."

In actual fact, excess of licence does at this period lead to weariness and distaste. The true gallant, the noble lover, is to disappear and give place to quite a new social type—the cavalier.

Previous to the formal reformation of old-time gallantry, profligacy, declares L'Estoile in his *Journal*, reached its highest point in the reign of Henri IV. "Debauchery and folly, ballets and lewd *divertissements*, duels and every form of impiety, were more than ever in the ascendency at this time." Under the last of the Valois sovereigns already "was the corruption such, that foolish buffoons, harlots and *minions* had all the credit. It was they disposed of all favors, and the tidbits of patronage." Le Gas, (the king's favorite) sold the Bishopric of Amiens to a court wench, one who had long been on the open market.*

Bassompierre relates in his interesting *Memoirs* how in 1606, by the advice of the ladies, he had a costume made for him for the completion of which "were required not less than fifty pounds of pearls. I wished it," he adds, "to be of violet-colored gold-tissue, with palm-branches interlacing. So, before leaving Paris, I —who had but seven hundred crowns in my purse— ordered a costume that was to cost me fourteen thousand crowns . . . to say nothing of a sword with a diamond hilt worth five thousand crowns†—total, something above 167,000 francs (£ 6680)!

This extravagant luxury, marking the transition from the age of gallantry to that of the cavalier, goes equally well with the early days of the latter period. The most shameless licentiousness is universally prevalent, and is to be seen even in the up-bringing of the sovereign's sons. To divert the young Dauphin (after-

---

* A little later, under Henri IV: "On Saturday the 12th of November" (1594), writes L'Estoile, "I was shown a handkerchief which a Parisian embroiderer had just finished for Madame de Liancourt, who was to carry it next day at a ballet, and had agreed with him on a price of 1700 crowns, which she was to pay to him in cash."—PIERRE DE L'ESTOILE, *Journal.*

wards Louis XIII), the great court-ladies used to sing softly to him various obscene ditties to relieve the premature melancholy of the young prince, tell him naughty tales, or else dance before him, with their lovers, the "Saint-Jean des Choux" (*St. John of the Cabbages*), the name of a coarse country dance, a dance in which each performer kicked the hind-quarters of the one, whether cavalier or lady, who was in front of him.

Further, it is found noted by Héroald* that to amuse this young scion of royalty, the same who in later life boasted of loving women only from the head to the waist, the most *advanced* nymphs of his circle used to delight in playing in his presence, *La Farce du badin mari* and *La femme garce et l'Amant qui la débauche* (The Farce of the Foolish Husband, The Enterprising Wife and the Lover who Seduces Her). Does not all this afford a pretty good idea of the morality and habits of the time—a transition period that has ceased to be precisely an epoch of gallantry, and not yet become, properly speaking, a cavalier one.

---

* JEAN HEROALD, *Journal sur l'enfance et la jeunesse de Louis XIII.* (Journal relating to the Childhood and Youth of Louis XIII) 1601-1628.

CHAPTER XII

France the Model of Fashion and Morals — Age of Cavaliers, Coxcombs and Swashbucklers

It is altogether beyond our powers to delineate his-torically all the different phases of degeneration affect-ing the Sword and the Sex simultaneously in each of the European nations. Accordingly, pursuing the same course as we have done for the epoch of *gallantry* and intend to do later on for that of the "fine gentlemen," we must limit our analysis of the manners and customs of the *cavalier* times to taking examples almost exclu-sively from old French life.

The world of France, always in old days mimicked by other nations, may very well by reason of this fact serve by itself to represent the distinctive social aspects which, under a gradual but constantly progressive degradation, have everywhere characterized modern life during the last three centuries.

The court of the Louvre, and subsequently that of Versailles, where little by little were elaborated the art of *gentilezza* (the gentle life) and the supreme refine-ment of vicious living, were in a special sense the scenes of the highest perfection of graceful manners. Elsewhere nothing beyond an insipid imitation at most was ever achieved.

Looking at a map of Europe, we may trace out the lines of delimitation bounding the regions of heavy sen, timentality by following with the finger the frontiers dividing the wine-countries from those where beer, the national beverage of the primitive Teutons, is the habit ual drink, which, Bismarck* declares, "makes men stupid, lazy and impotent."

In lands where malt and hops are brewed, martial spirit is cold and chill, love is without enthusiasm, intoxication itself without merriment. "Strong beer, tobacco that stings the tongue, and a servant-wench in her Sunday finery; those are the things I love." Here speaks the true German spirit in *Faust*, its repre sentative poem.

The regular beer-districts, none of which have ever yet produced graceful courtesans like Marion de Lorme nor nimble swordsmen like Miramont, draw their lines of demarcation between the Muscovite States, the an cient Slavonic provinces, whether Hungarian or subject to Turkey, that alluring region of Italy that embraces the plain of Lombardy and Venetia, and France, all jocund with her grape-clusters.

---

* At dinner (at Saint-Avold) the Councillors express a fear lest their favorite beverage, beer, should run short. "That is no loss," exclaims Herr von Bismarck. "The exces sive consumption of beer is deplorable. It makes men stupid, lazy and useless. It is responsible for the democratic non sense spouted over the tavern tables. A good rye whiskey is very much better."—Extract from Herr Moritz Busch's Book on Bismarck, Vol. I, p. 78 of the English edition, Macmillan, 1898.

In no country so well as in France has the art of arranging a duel fairly, been understood, courteously sharing sun, wind and position, of getting over a girl or cajoling a pretty woman, paying her favors with a song or serenade. "And this is why," say Béroalde de Verville,* "the German dames love the French far better than these heavy Germans," who make love like a whipped cur, and never take the initiative—as a witty Parisienne of more modern days has expressed it.

It was still just the same at Coblentz at the end of the eighteenth century—a fact which an exasperated critic of the time, Frederick Laukhard, confirms. "There is not left in that place," he declares, "a girl of 12 years old still virgin; the cursed Frenchmen coo so softly all men must blush at the results of their allurements. Girls, women, old and pious dames even, are intolerably given up to gallantry." To conclude, we find Napoleon's apothecary writing in his notes, about 1806: "Nothing can well be more complaisant or more loving than German women; they adore the French."

A nation that has produced Schopenhauer is of a surety not intended by nature for gallantry, or even for any agreeable form of dissoluteness. This Prussian satirist has expressed himself to the following effect in reference to women: "The intelligence of mankind," he writes, "must indeed have been obscured by love for them, ever to have given the name of the *fair sex*, the *beautiful sex*, to these creatures of puny

---

* BEROALDE DE VERVILLE, *Le Moyen de Parvenir.*

stature, narrow shoulders, wide hips and *short legs.*"
A phrase like this may be described as showing a want
of tact. A woman will allow herself to be told: you
belong to a sex possessing a small brain and a half-
developed organization; your disposition and instincts
are all disproportionate, inconsequent, hypocritical,
illogical and futile; your moral sense is deformed, your
selfishness without a scruple and your vanity without
a limit. All this will hardly so much as annoy her;
but dare to say: you have *short legs,* and you have committed a dire offence woman's nature can never forgive.
Further on, Schopenhauer adds another curiously in-
sulting passage: "The ancients," he says, "would have
laughed at our gallantry of the old French fashion
and our stupid veneration for *number two of the
human species;* a veneration which is merely the most
perfect realization of German-Christian silliness." Un-
doubtedly it is something—but it is by no means everything, to bring into the world like Augustus II., King
of Saxony, three hundred and fifty-four natural children.

From the same point of view, little need be said
of the "tall lads," the young men of sea-girt England, whom the Roman invasion found painted with
blue as late as in the days of Caesar.* They have
borrowed from France their motto and their National
Anthem† but never yet have they succeeded in catch-

---

* The Britons all stain the body a blue color. . . .
—CAESAR, *Commentaries,* bk. V., ch. 3.

† "It is a matter of common knowledge that the air and

ing our happy ways and tricks of manner, whether among gallants, cavaliers or mere men of pleasure. Lord Chesterfield is never weary, in his letters to his son, of exhorting the latter to imitate the French, as a means of rubbing off the Cambridge rust.*

The French King John, a love-lorn prisoner in England in the best days of the genuine *swordsmen*, and at a much later period the elegant Chevalier de Grammont, offered the nobility of Windsor and St. James perfect examples of the fascinating manners of their country. In olden times among the nation that practices the unceremonious *hand-shake*, before the days when *perfect gentlemen* had adopted the habit of driving away the lady guests from table before the dessert, such a thing as this was possible: a festival at which sixty English maidens leading on a leash like grey-

words of 'God save the King' are of French origin. When the most Christian King entered the Chapel Royal, the whole choir of the aforesaid noble damsels used to sing each time the following words to a very fine air composed by the Sieur Lully:

> Grand Dieu, sauvez le Roy!
> Grand Dieu, vengez le Roy!
> Vive le Roy!
> Que toujours glorieux,
> Louis victorieux
> Voye ses ennemis
> Toujours soumis!
> Grand Dieu, sauvez le Roy!
> Grand Dieu, vengez le Roy!
> Vive le Roy!"

—*Souvenirs of the Marquise de Créquy*, vol. I.

* *Letters of Lord Chesterfield to his son Philip Stanhope.*

hounds each a love-sick knight decorated with French mottoes. There likewise, in that land of fairy visions and the Queen of the Fairies, women have little by little lost their old prestige. I dare not here repeat what Lord Byron said of "young ladies."*

The descendants of Hengist and Horsa nowadays prefer their horses to the golden-haired *misses* of Albion, whose tender hands they roughly wring and shake up and down by way of salutation. And yet, in virtue of their very real charms, the blonde island beauties deserve a greater gentleness and courtesy.

In spite of the very real physical advantages of the English race with its complexion blent of the white carnation and the rose, the easy bearing of the true lady's man in fashion and *flirtation* hardly ever flourished in old days beyond the Channel except as a hot-house exotic—in other words, in the small world of the chosen few, and not always even there.

In 1716 the Princess Palatine, with that treacherous gentleness women practice towards one another—every woman instinctively hates every other—was delighted to record how Lady Sandwich, wife of the ambassador

---

* Lord Byron, writing to one of his friends, says: "Now think of the position of women under the ancient Greeks,— suitable enough. Present condition: a relic of the feudal bar- barity of the Middle Ages,—artificial and contrary to Nature. They should busy themselves with domestic matters; we should feed them well, and dress them well, but never bring them in contact with society. They should, again, be taught religion, but should know nothing of poetry or politics; their reading ought to be confined to books of devotion and cookery . . ."

of William III at the court of Louis XIV,* had been styled by the latter monarch on account of her quaint way of dressing her hair *the English ape,* which would seem to imply some inferiority at that epoch in Britannic grace and elegance.

It is then in virtue of a time-honored supremacy enjoyed by France in matters of breeding and fashion that we select that country, though now and again, incidentally citing some mode of Spain or Italy, as the main source from which to draw the special characteristics of the genuine *cavalier*-type of 1620 and thereabouts.

Pasquier writes in his book *Of the Origin of Words* "of *chevalier* (knight) we have made *cavalier,*" and the ladies might with truth claim to have done the same. The word *cavalier,*† whence we get the significant expression *"to treat cavalierly,"* summed up in its original acceptation for the female world of France, which was the social model to the rest of Europe, the

---

* "An unknown lady, a sort of English *monkey* (appears at court), wearing a little, low head-dress; in a moment the princesses fly from one extreme to the other." The *monkey* was Lady Sandwich, wife of the English ambassador. *Correspondence of the Duchesse d'Orléans* (the Princess Palatine), mother of the Regent.

Monkey was applied to signify a ridiculous looking person, ugly or ill dressed.

† *Cavalier,* a gentleman of birth who carries a sword. Is said also of a gallant who courts, who escorts a lady. . . . The same word is likewise used as an adjective, signifying free, easy, unconcerned. . . . Used also of anything *too free,* verging on incivility."—TREVOUX'S *Dictionary,* 1743.

ideal of all that was charming, of the "supreme mould of gallantry" in modes of speaking and making love.

Among *cavaliers* are to be counted men of "good bearing" in France, Spain and Italy; *coxcombs** dressed out in particolored satin, affecting the dainty wearing of lace collars and perfumed gloves, with *ladykiller* ruffs, gilt spurs, dancing plume and pearl earrings, carrying a Dutch tulip in their hands.

Among *cavaliers* are all the folk of riding-hood and sword, men of adventure in fight and love, whose pockets hold "a pack of cards, a set of dice and their little flute to make merry cheer withal"—fencers, pickers of quarrels, braggarts with their insolent looks and well-drawn hose.

To the same category belong the dandies or *marjolets*, "posers and vaporers," *pados* throwing perfumes and flowers to the ladies as they pass, *hidalgos* (noblemen, literally *sons of somebody*), *valentones* (braggarts), *diestros* (keen swordsmen), *matadores* or bullies, captains and *slitters of noses* who with arms a-kimbo, stiff back and straightened leg, wear their moustaches curled and twisted to the eyes,† their sword high tilted, sometimes carried without scabbard,‡ lifting

---

* *Coxcombs* are young men who pose as being in quest of adventures with ladies. . . . The coxcomb never goes in a straight line; that is too *common* for him."—FURETIERE'S *Dictionary*, under Maistre.

† *El bigote al ojo aunque no haya un cuarto*. (Moustachios curled up to the eyes, though he have not a cent).— QUEVEDO, *Obras escogidas* (Select Works).

‡ "Hat turned up behind, with a scalloped ruff round

in the Spanish mode the edge of mantle or great-cloak.

Mme. d'Aulnoy, in the reign of Charles II (of Spain), has given us a description of the costume of "a genuine Guap" (*guapo* or gallant)—a term synony-mous in the Spain of that day with braggadocio and *cavalier*—one of the formidable fellows whose rapiers with deep capacious basket-hilt were of such exag-gerated length of blade that they had to be carried in a special scabbard opening half way down with a spring that the wearer might be able to draw his weapon.

Without the sword, the Spanish type of the *alum-brado* (man intoxicated with love), the guitar-playing lover who pursues every woman, be she who she may, the Don Juan of the time, that easily pleased seducer of the *thousand and three*—the hero of rapid conquests, who is equally ready at a moment's notice to carry by assault noble ladies' hearts or to rumple a pretty chambermaid's neckerchief—without the sword such a type is impossible, and at this epoch women would have no other. "This is why, following the same turn of mind," says the old Spanish refrain, "a married woman's first thought and care is to devise how to be a widow."*

Mme. d'Aulnoy recorded in 1679: "A few days ago I was visiting the Marquise d'Alcañizas, one of the greatest ladies and most virtuous women of the

---

the neck, their swords very often without scabbard, mere-ly suspended by a cord."—MME. D'AULNOY, *Voyage d'Espagne*, vol. I.

* BRANTOME, *Dames galantes*, Fourth Discourse.

Spanish court. She said to us all openly, speaking
of love, 'I tell you frankly, if a cavalier had been half
an hour alone with me without asking me to grant
all a man can ask of a woman, I would feel so lively
a resentment against him that I would stab him, if I
could'." Mme. d'Aulnoy adds: "Few women but hold
the like views on this point."

If women of birth and high family thought and
spoke thus in the chivalrous land of Don Quixote,
what must not have been the thoughts, words and
works of contemporary beauties of easy virtue?—the
*bizarras** (gallant women), for instance, as they were
called in Madrid, where there were more than sixty
thousand in 1612, the frail charmers who publicly practiced the arts of gay caprice and gallant effrontery.

Such was the part which ladies of ease and leisure
assigned as a rule to *cavalier* advances, thus forcing
on their aspirants the enervating habit of facile pleasures, and making them as a consequence of progressive enfeeblement more and more apprehensive of
muscular fatigues.

An edict of Louis XIII in 1628 ordered all gentlemen
of birth, under pain of loss of rank, to wear for the
future defensive armor† in the field. The edict in
question and the regulations supplementing it produced no visible effect.

Long before this date, the rapier of the day, instru-

---

* AARSENS VON SOMMERDYCK, *Travels in Spain*, 1665.

† DANIEL, *Histoire de la Milice françoise* (History of
French Armaments), Amsterdam, 1724. Vol. VI, ch. I.

ment of the ruffler's and bully's triumphs, the weapon
of Cyrano de Bergerac and the d'Artagnans, grows
constantly more and more slender. More than ever is
it the indispensable accompaniment of the light intrigues
that relieve the monotony of war; and by its prestige
the cavalier stirs the hearts even of the country dames
amid the homage the latter loved to pay, for want of
a better object, to their ever complaisant patron, Saint
Guignolet.*

Cardinal Richelieu, after having donned a captain's
accoutrements at the siege of Rochelle, invariably
takes up the sword when he goes love-making; while
the very devil himself wears a long blade to dazzle
the girls, as was stated in evidence about the year
1640 in a criminal process directed against a young
witch-wife of Verberie.†

---

* "His falchion (the sword of Roland), which the chron-
iclers call his good sword Durandal, was conveyed to the
Church of Our Lady of Roquamadour or the Rock of Saint-
Amadour. It is related that Roland, visiting this chapel one
day, presented to the Virgin as much silver as equaled the
weight of his falchion. It is no doubt on this account the
said falchion was attributed to Our Lady of Roquamadour.
It was lost during the wars of the League; and the priests
replaced it by a heavy mass of iron, which continued to be
known as Roland's sword. The women of the district used to
go on pilgrimage to touch this falchion, to procure fertility."

† "Jeanne Herviller, of Verberie, near Compiègne, who
was condemned, as her mother had been before her, to be
burned alive, by judgment of the Parliament of Paris, confessed that her mother had presented her to the Devil under
the form of a tall man, black, and dressed in black, booted
and spurred, with a sword by his side and a black horse at the

Heart and soul devoted to "the flesh and the devil,"
when the highest praise a cavalier could receive was,
"He dances well! He is a handsome man! He has a
fine leg!"—all the world of gentlemen and lovers is
openly and avowedly the slave of ladies of the Sword
in close alliance with the young nobles of the *Fronde,*
of women of politics and of scholarly or scribbling
ladies reared at the same school of manners at which
Julie d'Angennes learned to glean the flowers of her
literary garland.

In the days of the wits, the Infanta Anne of Austria
imposed the fine manners and fashions of Spain on
the swordsmen of France, who still felt the effects of an
earlier Italian influence. Women with epistolary ambitions, ladies in quest of fine-drawn ideas or the pathos
of palpitating actualities, now set themselves to play
upon the romantic string in the already enervated
youth of the Sword. Love in its progressive weakness
is marked by excessive finical affectedness, and language
follows suit, under the auspices of the fine ladies, those
creatures of moods and vapors, who compromise the
cavaliers of high life and even the nobility of battle.

At the period which saw the martial triumphs of
the hero of Rocroy, the great Condé, who wept and
fainted on quitting Mlle. de Vigean* to join his army

door."—P. L. JACOB, *Curiosités de l'histoire des croyances
populaires* (Historical Curiosities of Popular Belief).

* "The great Condé was unable to say farewell to Mlle.
de Vigean without bursting into tears; and on starting for
his last expedition into Germany (from which he brought
back the victory of Nordlingen), he fainted away on the

in the field, a lover was said, in the fantastic diction of
ladies, always in search of startling contrasts, "to be
dying for his mistress," while in Spain they spoke of a
derretido (a man *melting* with love).* Judging by the
abandon of these expressions, we may gauge the effect
produced on the younger cavaliers, in other words, on
the aristocracy of that time by the influence of coquettes who, in accordance with the mode of the day,
used to write to their lovers in this strain: "I cannot
recall I have yet suffered you to write me; I could not
endure that you should speak to me."

The more distinguished, the more superior, among
the fine ladies, those who, in walking, swing the hips
in the Spanish fashion; those, who, to gratify their
vanity made their successful lovers fight under their
windows with the disappointed suitors, had striven to
establish as a principle that "love is not a mere passion
pure and simple, but a passion of necessity and polite
obligation; it behooves every man to be in love, and
every woman to be loved." "No man," say they,
"ought to be without love and without a mistress."
All this tended to set up a species of obligatory service
as due to all women alike.

In spite of these pretentions, pretensions stimulated
by the vogue enjoyed by the map of the *Pays du*

---

occasion of quitting her side."—*Memoirs,* vol. I, p. 85.—
VILLEMAIN, *La société française au XVIIe siècle* (French
Society in the Seventeenth Century), vol. I.

* TALLEMANT DES REAUX, *Historiettes,*—*Le marquis de
Rouillac.*

Tendre (Land of Love), nothing can really bring back the old illusions of an earlier day, even among such *cavaliers* and doughty knights as have undergone a preliminary sophistication at the Hôtel de Rambouillet. Into that home of culture, as a result of the unsatisfied caprices of the literary ladies, poetic creatures of the most superfine sensibility, left neglected by the gentle-men of their circle who are weary of their affectations and refuse to meet their advances, had already slipped sundry unpolished, *bourgeois* recruits like Voiture, who, wanting one day to warm his feet, made no ado about taking off his shoes in the princess's presence.

After the court, the most effectual instrument of perversion acting on the Sword was the world of the *salons.* "It may truly be said," writes Tallemant des Réaux in his *Historiettes,* "that Mme. de Rohan was one of the first and foremost to cause young men to lose the respect they formerly accorded to ladies; for to induce them to frequent her house constantly, she allowed them to take all conceivable liberties."

All true respect for women having thus little by little faded away, men of birth in their turn are now threatened with the loss of what is left of their old prestige. The jealousy of the Gown, constantly on the look-out to injure the Sword, had suddenly un-masked its batteries of hatred and ill-will, and Laffe-mas,* a creature of Richelieu, dares to have great

---

* "Laffemas is held to have been a sort of wholesale executioner and assassin. But it must be remembered he lived in a century when putting a nobleman to death was

lords beheaded.   The Duc de Boutteville in 1627 lost
his head simply for having fought a duel in defiance
of the prohibitions of the royal edicts.   This event, it
may be said without exaggeration, was the prologue
leading up by inevitable stages to the tragic finale
consummated in 1793.

---

a thing unknown, and Cardinal Richelieu made use of him
to give his first examples of its possibility."—TALLEMANT
DES REAUX, *Historiettes,*—265, Laffemas.

CHAPTER XIII

The Cavalier Grown Disreputable — Increasing Contempt for Women — Unnatural Vice

During the flourishing period of *cavalier* elegance, in the days when Cinq-Mars possessed three hundred pairs of boots, the majority of the lovelaces of the world of fashion, described as "apostates from good feeling," take to smoking tobacco and getting drunk. They lisp in speaking, frequent ill-reputed quarters of the town, gaming-houses and resorts of doubtful character, cheat at cards,* are swindled and robbed themselves, and snap their fingers at love. A large proportion revolt against all such claims, and defy the ladies, whom at the same time, with an affectation of the greatest politeness, they salute with bows to the very ground. The less corrupt exhaust themselves in flattering madrigals addressed to the fantastical fine ladies of high life or the Philamintas of the demi-monde. They beg for their heart's love in a set of verses, but, says Saint-Evremond, "they find much more pleasure in publishing abroad the favors their mistresses have conceded than in receiving them."

Towards the end of the same period a sermon of the Père de la Rue, attacking the vices of the time, insists

---

* Hamilton, *Memoirs of the Comte de Grammont.*

strongly on their influence "towards the enfeeblement of the military virtues by the corruption produced among young men."

Subsequently to the printing of the outspoken memoirs of Sully, no vestige of real sincerity, to speak generally—and always excepting Tallemant des Réaux and Rabutin—is to be found in the descriptions of French morality. The truth comes out only in the plain-speaking denunciations of the preachers.

Men of letters in the seventeenth century, living as they did almost invariably in Paris at the expense of their noble patrons, great lords and ladies, who lodged and pensioned them, could hardly be expected—not to mention the fact that they were subject to the royal censorship—to be anything but panegyrists of the court and society of their day. This accounts for the complaisant falsehoods published at this period, the false delicacy and pruderies of the romances and long-winded tales and the utterly fallacious ideas these have given currency to.

Books written from the time of Richelieu down to the *Fronde* as a rule represent the aristocracy of the period generally as summing up all that was most gentle and most honorable under the sun. But really, as a matter of fact, the *cavaliers* were in the highest degree depraved, while the women of this corrupt society had reached a point of absolute unbearableness in their glozing phraseology, their novel tricks and cajoleries and their falsity of heart.

They put on exaggerated airs of mock-modesty, and

assume a scornful pose before their admirers, all the
time longing to be noticed.

By virtue of such hypocrisies, matching well with
the mask women still wore, this period so full of con-
tradictions passes with present-day historians as having possessed every merit and every virtue. But there
is a reverse to this sham medal gilt only on one surface,
for plenty of foul meannesses are to be found in the
back-scenes of the great comedy of *cavalier* life amid
all the superabundance of dainty words. The illusion
still subsists among contemporary writers of optimistic
views who have read Mlle. de Scudéry's *Clélie;* but,
if between the years 1615 and 1699, we analyze a
little of what these authors delight in extolling, the
inexactitude of their insight into the manners of the
time is very soon apparent. During this vaunted
period "the ease with which women's favors could be
won—as well as their universal want of cleanliness*—
had made their charms so contemptible in the eyes of
young men that no one at court any longer so much
as thought of looking at them." This is what Bussy-
Rabutin† declares, at the same time accusing the *cava-*

---

* In the sixteenth century, in spite of the immoderate use
already made of perfumes, women were by no means always
sufficiently washed. In a love dialogue in the *Contes* of
Marguerite de Navarre, a lady avows "without any shame
that she has not cleansed her hands" for a week.—*Les Lois
de la galanterie française* (The Laws of French Gallantry,
1644). This book is well worth consulting on the subject of
this dirtiness in high life.

† BUSSY-RABUTIN, *Histoire amoureuse des Gaules.*

liers of his day of indulgence in unnatural vice—a vice
women usually condone with an inexplicable compla-
cency.

As another proof of the general contempt women
now inspired may be mentioned the rapid decrease,
and eventually the entire suppression, of those symbols
of admiration and flattery which did honor to their
sex and their beauty, in olden days the objects of such
fervent worship. These symbols, which for centuries
had adorned everything, even down to the very busk
of a lady's corset, totally disappeared in the course of
a few years.

In the ages of primitive chivalry which made woman
into a goddess, the motto of the Sword was ever "God
and my lady!" A little later a variant is found, "God
and fair ladies!" Here is the gallantry of the senses
already showing the point of its satyr's ear. Concurrently as licence increases, is God eclipsed in the
mottos by love; while last of all love itself disappears,
giving place to the king. Watching these successive
changes, accompanied as they were by greater and
greater laxity of military honor and fealty, we should
be justified in saying that women while losing their
own repute, have robbed the Sword one by one of each
and all of its best beliefs.

In the golden age of chivalric respect for women,
lovers walking with their ladies used to support the
latter with a hand under the arm. This protecting
and loving gesture which is represented in old miniatures and tapestry, would seem to have ceased abruptly

towards the middle of the fifteenth century. From that
date onwards, monuments and other works of art,
invariably, whatever the subject may be, represent
women clad as lightly as possible and posed in caressing attitudes, as much as to say to their male compan-
ion: "Don't go away!"

Other observations of a different character prove
that simultaneously with the decline of the Sword, the
last fragments of feminine prestige fall of themselves
like the walls of Jericho—not that this in any way hin-
dered the gallantries of the Renaissance period making
a brave and vigorous show.

To return to the men of the sword of the seventeenth century. By force of habit they are still submissive to women's caprice; and adopt in love-making
the new affected fashions prescribed by them, but
while yielding obedience to their will, they are all the
while far from granting them the high importance
of an earlier day.

Without going into too minute and for that reason
possibly unseemly details, it is easy to gather that
gentlemen of the *cavalier* days set themselves deliberately to disdain, to slight the ladies, and even to abuse
them, letting pamphleteers and preachers indulge in
public invectives against them. Under Louis XIV,
Bossuet and the Père de la Rue used in their sermons
habitually to scold and insult the high-born ladies of
literary pretensions and affectations.

Then, as we have seen above, were produced once
again in the history of manners abnormal effects re-

versing all established principles of women's habits.
The latter are eager to recall the old-fashioned love
now turned into contempt; but it is too late. This fact
they realize with grief and anger. Making trial of a
method imported from Italy, they are for ever indulg-
ing in the *vapors,* and having as a last resource grown
prudish, though in words only, they merely succeed
in becoming altogether insupportable, and are rele-
gated to separate beds. In the Middle Ages one bed
alone sufficed for husband and wife; but the habit of
sleeping together will be found pretty generally preter-
mitted at this period among gentlefolks.

Italians of good birth and breeding, grown indifferent, finally renounce their time-honored jealousy. The
greater part tolerate the *cicisbéo* as a part of family
life, while some husbands, disgusted with women altogether, actually end by addressing to the Pope an
abominable petition with a view to obtaining an authorization from him to have dealings with the other sex
during the summer.* Among the Germans, too, the
same kind of repugnance for all things feminine arises.
As to the Spaniards, repentant of having ever invented
the alcove, which at night brought them into the clos-
est contact with their *better half,* they follow the practice of sleeping alone as much as possible.

---

* "A similar petition had before this time been addressed
to Pope Sixtus IV (1471-1484), to gain permission to
commit the offence against Nature during the months of
oppressive summer heat. Sixtus wrote at the bottom of the
petition: "Let it be done as desired by our petitioners."—
History of France, by the Abbé Velly, vol. V., p. 10.

Already public satires directed against coquettes grow more numerous and more bitter, but above all in the good town of Paris do epigrams dealing with their misdemeanors abound. Against these manifestations of disfavor, so wounding to the sex and particularly to the more high-born members of it, the more important of them only set fresh extravagances, in the effort to regain their influence over the sword by the institution of systematic immorality.

After being duelists, leaders of coteries and political intrigues, Captains or Major-Generals in the army of Mlle. d'Orléans,* and later conspirators of the opposition, in the days when Mme. de Longueville took military possession of the little town of Stenay, the ladies of France, always a model to the other women of Europe, set themselves to exert what is left of their influence on the crowd of cosmopolitan Bohemians and the ranks of men of looks, these latter already getting rare.

Giddily following their ambiguous mode of existence, hardly conscious of their true bearings, they pretty gen-

---

* "There was a Regiment raised under the name of *Mademoiselle's* troop, and Monsieur actually wrote to women who had followed his daughter to Orléans in these terms: To my lady Countesses, Major-Generalesses in my daughter's Army against Mazarin."—Abbé THOMAS, *Essai sur le caractère des femmes* (Essay on the Character of Women), 1771.

The highest and noblest Amazon in the world, the Empress of Austria, received in 1881 a singular compliment and one of quite a feudal type, the Emperor of Russia having conferred on her the title of Honorary Colonel of a Regiment of Uhlans.

erally betake themselves at last to mere plunder and
thievery, while their lovers, victims of indifference and
lassitude, strike work for good and all, and the sword
gets ever smaller and ever weaker.

Presently the nymphs of the final revels, Adriane,
Dorille, Mélitée, Sylvanthe, Nérinde, Orinthie,* those
faded beauties, destined to have as descendants the
merveilleuses of the libertine age, do like the fair lady
of Saint-Eustache, who, so said the people, preferred
the first comer as a lover.

Such is everywhere the behavior of the greatest
ladies, too clearly betraying their utter depravity of
morals.

Mme. de Chevreuse delights in hearing Boisrobert's
filthy works read aloud, while the honorable and
learned Christina of Sweden, whom Colbert was
charged with the task of looking after for fear she
should pilfer some valuable during her visit to the *palais
Mazarin,*† makes her young favorite, Mlle. de Sparre,

---

*Adriane, Dorille, Mélitée, Sylvanthe, Nérinde and Orin-
thie, the Nymphs of the Revels of 1640.—VULSON DE LA
COLOMBIERE, *Théâtre d'honneur et de chevalerie,* vol. IV.

Again in 1686 there was another sham feast of chivalry,
a *rococo* masquerade, known as the Revels of the gallant
Moors, at which the most dancing-mad of all great kings
of France figured. He was pleased to perform before the
court in the costume of Apollo or Alexander the Great with
a flowing wig and naked limbs.

† "The Queen of Sweden did not see Your Eminence's
apartments in the Louvre. . . . If she had visited them, I
should have endeavored to prevent irregularities, as I did,
with no little difficulty, in Your Eminence's Palace, albeit

read out before Saumaise certain dirty French stories.*
It is well known how this stalwart and gallant queen,
after her debauches with Swedes and Spaniards of
Brussels, had her ex-lover, Monaldeschi,† killed almost
before her very eyes at Fontainebleau. He had succeeded to the hard place of lover to that *exigeante*
princess in lieu of Magnus de la Garde, and had just
been himself supplanted by François Sentinelli, who
likewise soon had a series of successors.

M. de la Bretesche, who was on guard with Her Majesty,
did all I desired of him."—*Lettres originales et Mémoires
de Colbert au cardinal Mazarin*, Paris, Sept. 15, 1656.

* "During the time when Saumaise lay ill at the court
of Sweden, Queen Christina, who had induced him to visit
that country, went to see him, and found him in bed and
reading a book, which out of respect he closed the instant
he saw her enter. She asked him what it was. He confessed
it was a book of somewhat loose tales, which in the inter-
vals of his sickness he was reading for amusement.   'Ha,
ha!' said the Queen; 'come, let's see what it's like, show
me one of the good places.'   Saumaise having shown her
one of the best, she first of all read it through to herself,
smiling.   Then, to afford herself still greater pleasure, she
cried, addressing the beautiful Mlle. Sparre, her favorite, who
understood French: 'Look, Sparre, look what a charming
book of devotion, called the *Moyen de parvenir!* Now, read
me out that page aloud!' "

† "Account of the Marquis de Monaldeschi, Grand Equerry
of Queen Christina of Sweden, put to death by order of said
Queen, November 10th, 1657,—written by Père le Bel,
Minister of the Congregation of Mathurine Monks at Fontainebleau, who was the sole witness of the execution in
question."—Abbé GUILBERT, *Description hist. de Fontainebleau* (Historical Description of Fontainebleau), Paris, 1731.

In the following century Catherine II of Russia showed no less depravity of character, but at any rate this latter was not cruel, for it is an ascertained fact that to maintain and support in luxury her sixteen principal lovers she expended four hundred and ninety-one millions of francs,* a sum representing more than a milliard (a thousand millions) of the money of our day.

In view of the behavior and morals of these two queens, the general conduct of the Swedish and Russian ladies of those days may be conjectured, at a period when their sovereign was the undisputed arbiter of all feminine fashions and modes of life.

The morals of women in the seventeenth century, and this in spite of the praises lavished on them by the great panegyrists of love, display in the midst of European civilization many other revolting particulars, and those of Frenchwomen among the first and foremost. Bayle writing from Rotterdam in 1695, à propos of a new book, says: "This work, as well as several others reaching us from France, gives us a strange picture of the Parisian ladies. These have grown, we are told, into great drinkers of brandy and great takers of snuff, not to mention the other excesses they are accused of, such as gallantry, ill-natured backbiting and immodesty." They offend in "over-eating, the use of tobacco, hot cordials and too much wine," is the

---

* Casteras, *Life of Catherine II.*

Masson, *Mémoires secrets sur la Russie* (Secret Memoirs of life in Russia.

reiterated complaint of contemporary observers; this will give some idea of the rest of their faults. At Stockholm, at Copenhagen, the "fair sex" copies and exaggerates the French vices.   In Teutonic countries in the same century noble German ladies of every age, girls and matrons alike, drink beer in bumpers to intoxication, give their favors by sheer wanton complaisance, or, as a refined pastime, shoot at a mark. As to their fellow-countrywomen, merry dames of lower pretensions, they likewise, "living such ill lives it were impossible to be worse," have by their profligate ways exerted a highly disastrous influence over the military character of their compatriots.

"Beyond the Rhine," Sommerdyck writes in 1655,* "women get drunk almost as much as beyond the Pyrenees." They do so much more, if we are to credit the

---

* "I will say this, that in Germany I have not seen quite so many women who got drunk as I met on this side of the Pyrenees."—AARSENS VAN SOMMERDYCK, *Travels in Spain,* 1654.

In connection with the drunken habits of ladies in the seventeenth century, habits which continued in fashion long after its termination, we will quote some passages from the letters of the Princess Palatine, the mother of the Regent. In a letter dated May 7, 1696, she says:

"My son's wife is a disgusting creature; she gets as drunk as a bellman three or four times a week."

Later on, in a letter dated from Versailles, April 29, 1704, we read: "Intoxication is only too much in fashion among young women."

Lastly, Aug. 15, 1719, she writes, speaking of Mme. de Parabère: "She would be very tolerable if she were not so much given over to drunkenness."

English Ambassador then resident in Prussia. Such is the behavior of women generally in the seventeenth century, from Madrid to Moscow.

Ladies of quality—such was the name given of old, to the fashionable women of high life—passed on their vicious tastes and artificial manners to their *bourgeois* neighbors. "Cranes when they migrate," says Saint Jerome, "always follow a leader crane that guides all the rest." And it is the same with women and their fashions.

In every town in Europe, the Cathos and Madelons with that pretentiousness and grotesque folly that is characteristic of the class, made a point of mimicking, while envying all the while, the *fashionables,* court favorites and great ladies; just as these latter have invariably taken a delight, ever since from the days when St. Boniface rebuked them, in imitating the popular courtesans of the day.

Thus by a sort of contagion patrician dames made their *bourgeois* sisters arrogant and luxurious, and eventually immoral. As early as 1220, rich German ladies, at Mainz, entering into open competition with the fair charmers of the aristocracy, wore dresses with trains, in defiance of the reproaches the preachers directed against them from the pulpit.

The low moral tone of noble ladies in these days had the further evil of ruining by force of bad example not only the middle classes, but the lower orders as well.

"It is the chamber-maids that give the dogs fleas,"

was a significant phrase of the Sire de Canaples, brother to the Marquise de Créquy.

Thus in the seventeenth century do we find the moral sense of the men of the Sword more and more astray under the influence of the women of the period. Married women of the magisterial and merchant classes, who were in France expressly forbidden by law to wear velvet or silk, but who nevertheless "are clothed like princesses," get money from whomever they can, always provided it is not their husbands, to seduce and keep gallant musketeers as their lovers, who but for that would have refused them flatly. "No more love without pay," say the lower type of rufflers of the day; their ideas are not bound by any very high standard, and they become in these days the avowed purveyors of sensual delights. To buy brave attire, "for lack of better, they put up with old women's superannuated charms"; they sell lascivious dreams and sophisticated joys to garrison charmers, impatient wantons and uncomely but sturdy dames who have no longer either time or right to make difficulties.

"There is a class," says La Bruyère, "of women who are past their prime and whom their evil character make the regular resource of young men ill supplied with the world's goods." "I really do not know which is the most to be pitied," he goes on, "a woman of a certain age who needs a lover or a man who needs a superannuated mistress." Brantôme had already in his time spoken in his *Dames galantes* of "the love of sundry ladies of ripe age."

These shameful practices, so discreditable to the honor of the Sword, prevailing among the younger members of the military caste, recall the very ancient national song of Brittany known as the *Ann hani goz,* —*E va dous,* the words of which run thus, in a literal translation:

"I have an old woman for sweetheart,
    My sweetheart is old for sure;
Yet the while I am dreaming of a young maid I love.
    The young maid is fair indeed,
    But the old dame has money."*

Such is the way of the world of cavaliers and ruffling gallants; it is still, and more than ever, true that between dashing dames of fashion and men of the rapier self-interest and pleasure are the two great bonds of union. These two baits never fail to catch the vast majority of the king's good soldiers, who keep garrison in country towns, where they find nothing in the way of amusement but intrigues or else downright debauchery. Their stay is the delight at once of mistresses and servant-maids, entranced by the dashing figures of the soldiers, their gay uniforms and military music. After all nothing can be more natural. To realize today the effect produced in old times, it is quite enough to watch the arrival of a squadron of cavalry or a regiment of the line in a small provincial town. The way

---

* *Les Caquets de l'accouchée* (Gossip of the Lying-in Room), 1623: "They are forced to make love to an old woman or to cajole the daughter of a rich house. Only base-born brats and seduced girls are to be found."

the ladies, and all their maids and abigails, crowd the windows with open eyes, gives no bad idea of the attraction exercised in the times of gallant and handsome cavaliers by the swagger of men of the Sword, flashing their dazzling blades so bravely in the sun.

"Une autre ville, une autre fille."

(Another town, another mistress.)

are the words of a very old song.   Thus was the heterogeneous admixture of races by selection carried on through the gallantry and intrigues of the Sword, whose bastards were indeed held in relatively high esteem.

To such scandalous circumstances did many a little *bourgeois* and peasant owe his birth, children whose good looks and delicate hands and feet betray the faults, or let us say the venial caprices, of their mothers.

Observe once more how women, who are always attracted by *ne'er-do-wells* and scamps (in France a *mauvais sujet* is rather admired than otherwise), preferred as a rule to an honest professional man or tradesman some red-coated Adonis with sword at side.   The rapier indeed was, in imitation of the Spanish mode,*

---

* "At the Assembly of the Estates at Paleccia, the Emperor Charles the Fifth, among other ordinances there promulgated, forbade any to appear masked in public, in order to deprive malefactors of the means of concealment; at the same time leave was given to all persons to wear the sword, to the end that men of low estate might be able to defend themselves in case of attack; but the privilege of the nobility granted to common people made the latter proud and idle. . . ."—

worn with impunity down to 1660 by *scaramouches*
and street braggarts, till it was at last forbidden by
royal edict to men of low birth. "A young man of
middling condition, a Parisian, who never went abroad
without a great sword at his side, made much play with
the girls of his quarter, and brought some of them into
evil case," relates Tallemant des Réaux. All the gay
fellows, the Lotharios and the very lackeys, in Paris,
in imitation of those of Madrid, carried the long
sword; only towards the end of the *cavalier* period they
avoided, in consequence of a long-delayed edict of
prohibition, passing over the Pont-Neuf, where the
police-officers had orders to impound their weapon.
The arm of nobles has indeed fallen low!

At the same time that Boileau is launching his invectives against women in his Discourses, Molière at
his sovereign's instigation dares to mock at the sword
on the stage. It is now fallen on evil days, and he
takes full advantage of the fact. A threat with the
Great King's walking-stick was to show it that under
certain circumstances it could incur humiliation and
even ridicule. Yet from the days of fabulous legend
downwards any such supposition seemed utterly inad-
missible, even when Mars lay caught like a fish in the
net by Vulcan. Now, the confident pride of the aristocracy once troubled, the chagrined swordsmen begin
one fine day to visit the blame on the ladies.

Abrégé chron. de l'histoire d'Espagne et de Portugal (Chronological Summary of the History of Spain and Portugal),
vol. II, Paris, 1765.

From 1620 and onwards, there is perceptible, stirring the perfumed air of their dainty world, suspicions of the critical attitude, threats, even spurts of mocking laughter against women.

The seventeenth century, rough and cavalier in spite of all its high pretence of sentimental tenderness and its romances, made good use of the birch, or to adopt the language of the period, caressed with the disciplinary switch, its dulcet dames, its affected *précieuses*. Queen's favorites and even queens themselves, all submit, and occasionally, like the wife of Sganarelle, or the Egyptian lady in *Zadig*, they take a positive pleasure in being whacked. The number of those who endured such treatment is considerable. Mme. de Montbazon was all but beaten by d'Hocquincourt, and Buckingham boasted of having, in the quality of their lover, *drubbed* three queens, the queen of France being one.

Mme. de Rohan, Tallemant des Réaux relates, always had the aspiration of being beaten by her lovers. "They say she liked it." "To be beaten is not a privilege every woman can command," the Marquise de Blainville would remark regretfully. Fashion having once sanctioned this pre-eminently *cavalier* way of treating ladies, Monsieur the King's brother by way of affording a good example, boxes Mlle. de Beauvais' ears at a ball.* It is notorious how M. de Lauzun ill-

---

* "The king's brother the other day, at a certain court ball, . . . fell and hurt himself; and getting up again full of vexation, he heard Mlle. de Beauvais give a loud laugh. This seemed to him so ill-natured that he suddenly ran up to

used Mademoiselle the King's eldest daughter, who later on was copied in certain forms of indulgence by the lascivious Duchesse de Berry, the same whom M. de Riom, lieutenant of Dragoons, compelled to pull off his boots.

What a contrast these coarse brutalities present to the old world tenderness of chivalrous days!

In the reign of Louis XIV, the constant state of war which lasted for twenty years did not stop a certain amount of love-making.   But as the court was filled with old unimpressionable cavaliers, or else with young men rendered brutal by their trade of arms . . . the ladies, not to lack caresses altogether, grew as a rule compassionate to suitors and some utterly shameless.   All essayed to seduce the king.   Failing success in that quarter, such as longed for sensual gratifications consoled themselves elsewhere, holding that in this respect the sovereign might be replaced by some mean person of the lowest condition, one who could be readily changed on occasion.   It was not long before they began to run after men—the reason many scorned their charms altogether.   These are the words of a contemporary of the *dames précieuses,* who in conjunction with the youth of the Sword, gave the seventeenth century its most characteristic aspects.

---

her, and losing all respect for the young girl, applied a blow to her tender cheek, that sounded clearly through the room."
—J. DE LORET, *Muse historique: Recueil de lettres en vers écrites à Mlle. de Longueville* (The Muse of History,—a Collection of Letters in Verse written to Mlle. de Longueville).

The fact cannot but be recognized that at this date women in the domain of the senses have met with a check. Their design was to provoke a reaction, but in this they failed. Seeing this, the dandies of the day made it their boast to depreciate and belittle women, even before the latter had given them their first opportunity of knowing and compromising them.

Here is the final degradation of the Sword as representative of the soldier, to have done with the *cavalier* who is now to change his nature completely and degenerate into the weakling libertine pure and simple.

Through the fault of women of luxurious and self-indulgent life whose pleasure was to make him dance attendance on them and be for ever providing them with music and collations, the cavalier is finally reduced to the condition and dignity of a mere running footman. He is merely, to use the diction of the drawing-rooms of to-day, a person of no importance, a valser, a creature to make up a quadrille or a cotillon.

In connection with these Italian modes, wherein we see gentlemen, in spite of all their disreputable adventures and nocturnal duels, again beginning to pay scant heed to women and their claims, it is to be remarked that with the expiration of the *cavalier* period, jealousy on the part of husbands is quite out of fashion and the ancient code of vengeance abrogated. If rival lovers still at times roused the town, it was far more out of vanity than for love. The great majority of husbands in those days tolerated only too gladly a deputy alongside their wives.

Such indifference to the behavior of the so-called amiable sex and to the true point of honor shows plainly to what an extent notions of loving tenderness and moral obligation had been degraded among the higher classes since the days of gallantry, when jealous spouses would kill their wives on a mere suspicion of falseness.

This apathetic tolerance can be more and more clearly verified in proportion as the evidence comes nearer to our own time, and thus affords more and more conclusive proofs.

CHAPTER XIV

EVIL PRACTISES OF LIBERTINISM—HOT-BEDS OF
DEBAUCHERY—ROUES, LADIES OF QUALITY,
AND GENERAL ORGIES

Towards the end of the great reign of that king of
pedants, Louis XIV, a period so hugely overpraised
that we forget its absurdities, its last years of failure
and defeat and even its bankruptcy to the tune of two
thousand million francs, the Sword undergoes an entire
metamorphosis in its character as representative of its
wearers, in the importance of the rôle it plays and in
its shape and aspect as a weapon.

Before the death of the "Roi-Soleil," as he was
called, who began by dancing in a cuirasse of gold,
with limbs naked and an enormous curled wig, in the
court-ballets, and on campaign had ten assorted enemas
administered on the eve and on the days of battle,*

---

* The Royal Library contains a burlesque solemn memo-
randum of the victories and dysenteries of Louis XIV. The
original MS. in question (Supplément français, No. 1271)
was given to the Royal Library by M. Hulst, who acquired
it from Mme. de Verrejon, heiress of M. Fagon, son of the
famous king's physician, a Councillor of State and who died
in 1744. It is a small folio, written on paper, with a
binding adorned with fleurs-de-lis. At the beginning are
two fine portraits of Louis XIV, engraved by Rousselet and
van Schuppen, after Lebrun and Mignard.

"The Spanish army lay some quarter of a league distant

and ended by marrying a nursemaid, the gilded youth
of the Sword, with or without the assistance of the
ladies, devotes itself to every sort of disorder and debauch, showing in this way its defiance of "the old
dame of St. Cyr" (Mme. de Maintenon), chief patron-

from the French out-posts; and this army, under the command of the Prince de Condé, seemed superior to that of
Turenne, who had quite made up his mind not to risk a
general engagement.   Well, the king at this juncture arrived
in Turenne's camp in a condition which Vallot used to at-
tribute to an over-indulgence in lemonade rather than to the
nearness of the foe.   'As the trouble was increasing,' relates
the eye-witness we have mentioned, 'I was compelled at
Montmédi to administer an enema, the king dismounting, but
still all booted, and in a spot surely the most desolate and
most inconvenient in the kingdom.   The effect of this remedy
restored the king to some degree of strength and spirit; so
that next morning he set forth to continue his designs and
pursue his march.'

"The young king, in spite of the ambulatory treatment
he submitted to with so much good-will, could not remain
beyond five days in the camp, during which the Spaniards
made some smart attacks; he then returned to Paris to complete his cure.

"Mazarin brought him once more to the army in September, to have him present at the siege of Sainte-Menehould,
and lo! the plaguey diarrhœa beginning afresh.

"But this time Vallot, who was not a whit behind Molière's
Purgon, devised a radical treatment which the king followed
out, without giving up riding every day and proceeding with
his great undertakings.   The treatment consisted in ten clys-
ters of different sorts.   No less was needed to keep up the
king's vigor, who now scarce ever left the saddle, and who
forced the besieged to surrender, says the surgeon in his account,—which they would not have done so soon, had not
his Majesty been present at the cost of personal suffering."—
P. L. JACOB, Curiosités de l'histoire de France, Paris, 1858.

ess of the sham religious reverence among womankind.*

In that vast palace of Versailles which had cost
France a hundred and fifty-three millions, before the
gold-braided coat of the king, which cost him twelve
million five hundred thousand francs,† and which he
had had made to receive a pretended ambassador from
Persia, the Sword hangs its head in discomfiture and
humiliation.   The aristocracy loses its ancient pride

---

* Her pet rôle.   She thought herself a mother of the
church and general directress of consciences for the court.
The meanness and poverty of her earlier life had narrowed
her mind and spoiled her finer feelings to such a degree that
all her life she was so small and petty in her ways of thinking
as to be below the level even of a Madame Scarron.   Nothing
more repulsive than this baseness of spirit in combination with
so radiant a position, and nothing so destructive of good,
nothing so inconvenient and actually dangerous, as this continual vacillation with regard to men and affairs.   Further she
had the *foible* of allowing herself to be influenced by the
confidences, better still by the confessions, she extracted."—
SAINT-SIMON, *Mémoires.*

Versailles, April 19, 1701. . . . "The king is more attached than ever to *his dirt.*"   Such is the designation the
Princess Palatine gives to Mme. de Maintenon.   In the
course of the same letter we find twice over this title of *old
filth* applied to Mme. de Maintenon.   In other letters again
it is "the old slop."

† Louis XIV, though no longer a young man, wore at the
reception of an ambassador from the king of Persia a coat of
a material of gold and watered silk embroidered with diamonds, worth several millions (about twelve millions five
hundred thousand francs).   It was so heavy that, says Dan-
geau, the king "was in a hurry to put it off after the cere-
mony was over."

and submits to the yoke of the imposing despot, while
the ladies of fine manners, wearied of the insipid etiquette he enforces, give full rein to frivolity and dissipation.   Just as in preceding periods they had pro-
the advent of a generation *blasé* with love, we shall
find them encouraging the most inordinate and extravagant license of morals.   This is the way by which they
reach their predetermined goal, viz., by an occult and
furtive domination of the Sword resulting in its complete and final subjection to the sensual element in
woman.   This new system of behavior they had originated from the earliest maturity of the *Great* King,
at the time of the first Versailles fêtes.   "Divertissements by day, walks and feastings lasting till two and
three in the morning, in the woods, were carried out in
a fashion of *something more than gallantry,*" writes
Mme. de Motteville.

This fashion *of something more than gallantry* is
the germ of that modish dissipation which only reaches
its highest completion at the commencement of the Regency.   The mere word indeed of *The Regency* awakes
in the imagination ideas of strange, wild obscenities and
nocturnal orgies.   From the general debauchery of
those years, debauchery which women do their best to
stimulate, issue fully equipped for their tasks, the *roués,*
the characteristic figures of the new epoch.

In the opinion of Jean-Jacques Rousseau the profligacy of his epoch was the inevitable consequence of
the influence of women, for that gentle philosopher

maintains men will always be what the women wish them to be. In very fact women make "fashion that is stronger than any law." This undoubted fact would alone suffice to justify the philosopher's complaint.

"I am deliberately of the opinion," wrote Cardinal de Bernis* in his *Memoirs*, "that intercourse with wo-

---

* "I am deliberately of the opinion that intercourse with women has changed French character and habits. In for- mer days gentlemen were admitted to their society at earliest at thirty; till that age men lived with men. This made their spirit more masculine and their principles more firm. Nowa- days it is women who teach men to think; at seventeen, and sometimes even younger they enter the world. At that age it is but natural to regard the being agreeable to the ladies as the main point of all; and young men are accustomed from the first to idleness, effeminacy and frivolity, coming eventually to the business of life with empty heads and hearts crammed with false ideals. . . .

"From what I say it may be judged how different are the great lords of today from those of old times; with less credit and wealth than in the reigns of Louis XIII and Henry IV., they also have less dignity and prestige than under Louis XIV. Their expenses are heavy; they love money, and do not blush to ask for it, and sometimes to receive it. At the same time the use they put it to can be no excuse for the generally embarrassed condition of their affairs. They display vanity, but legitimate pride never."—Cardinal de BERNIS, *Mémoires*.

The following description of a *Petit-Maître*, or Dandy, about the year 1730, will give some idea of the depth of effeminacy to which feminine influence had brought the youth of the Sword: "Here we have the *Petit-Maître* represented attiring himself with much care, and then running to his mir- ror, standing before which he gazes at his own face, of which he is the only admirer. Next we have him at his toilette table, where he applies patches and rouge to his cheeks, where his hair is put through the curling-irons, having the evening

men has changed French character and habit." There can be no doubt as to the transformation being their work—the change from the ways and bearing of the *cavalier,* still imbued with some tincture of the ancient gallantry, into the evil fashions and vicious practices of the *man of pleasure;* there can be no doubt as to their being responsible for the utter degradation of the Sword and the tragic catastrophe of the good old times.

Diderot, a disappointed lover, if we may judge by certain of his Works and Letters, has depicted after Nature the vicious man of rank according to the mode of 1760. "The man of pleasure," he says, "is gay, witty, dissipated, an amateur of every pleasure. . . ." And lower down he adds, "Women love the libertine man of pleasure because they are libertines them-selves."* This is sufficiently plain speaking surely!

----

before been twisted in curl-papers, and his hair is artfully combed, powdered and scented."—*Journal des Savants,* 12mo, Dec., 1732, pp. 2159, 2160. Again further on: "We see the same *Petit-Maître* well powdered and scented, dressed in a close-fitting coat glittering with gold and silver, with a waist-coat of equal splendor adorned with heavy bullion fringe; this is the fashion, and he is bound to follow it. Then he may be seen sallying out, looking himself over from head to foot, admiring all his person, stepping as if on air, bending gently over, now to one side, now to the other, continually, putting up his hand to his hair for fear a lock should be disarranged, gazing round to see if folks are not all enchanted at so charm-ing a vision,—and all the rest of it. . . ."—TREVOUX, *Dict. de la langue française,* see under *Petit-Maître.*

* The men of pleasure are well received in society because they are light-hearted, gay, witty, dissipated, easy-going, ama-teurs of every pleasure. . . . Women love them, because they

These libertines, whether *of condition* or *of quality* (there was still a difference of meaning in the exact significance of the two expressions), entered into rivalry with the most adept courtesans and adapted themselves in these days to the entirely sensual part they had elected to play.

As a rule *mignonnes* are plump, with dimples in chin, cheeks, and knees and a spot considerably lower down than the shoulders—thus their poets and painters, such as were really admitted to their intimacy, delineate them. Full of affectation from head to foot, "dressed to kill," bedizened and bepainted more elaborately than so many Nürnberg dolls—a patch at the corner of the eye, eyes demurely dropped, lips smiling and moist as a peach bursting with ripeness—they displayed above a low-cut and gaping corsage in which was stuck a rose exhaling its dying perfume, their bosom naked and set off to the utmost advantage, an enticing specimen of other dainties below. Such was the physical type essentially characteristic of ladies of society in the days of modish libertinism now dawning.

To match the new seductions, the new modes and fashions of love, gentlemen were bound to assimilate their costume, their manners and their effrontery to those of their charmers. Accordingly we see them represented in miniatures and contemporary portraits all powdered, and decked out, wearing embroidered coats,

---

are themselves libertines and pleasure-lovers. I am far from sure whether women are really displeased with men who make them blush."—DIDEROT, *Pensées,*—On Men of Pleasure.

carrying a mere suspicion of a sword at their side and
in their face a mere suggestion of the debauchee. Each
seems to be saying with a simper of carmined lips the
same self-satisfied words, "Look at me! I am Prince
Prettyman."

All these ludicrous effects follow from a want of
steady principle, a light *insouciance* of character; and
simultaneously the *cartel* with its slender, flexible blade,
the miniature sword of an over elaborated civilization,
now carries its process of degeneration in the direction
of greater and greater slenderness and lightness to the
highest degree—and this not in France alone, but everywhere else in Europe as well. The man of quality,
conscious of his utter enfeeblement, practices the graceful art of fencing. More than ever does the art now
reach a high perfection of swift and cunning movement, according to the latest mode of the Parisian
fencing-masters, who in this country gained the privilege of ennoblement after following their profession
for twenty years.*

While men of the Sword are thus mainly taken up
with the suppleness of their muscles and the shape of
their legs, their time shared between a fencing-master
and a teacher of dancing, the conduct of war becomes
finical in the extreme. The Marquise de Pompadour
dictates the plans of a campaign.† A band of actors

---

* In the eighteenth century the fencing-masters of Paris
established an Academy of Fencing consisting of twenty of
their number.

† "Mme. de Pompadour, writing to Marshal d'Estrées,

plays in camp, and Mme. Favart, on the eve of a general engagement, announces to the soldiers the orders for the day in a set of verses.

War, long since made ridiculous, "is now conducted," in the phrase of a contemporary letter-writer, "only with rose-water."* The day on which the Prince de Soubise was defeated (in September, 1757), "his camp was found filled with a host of cooks, comedians, hair-dressers, numberless parrots and parasols and I cannot tell how many cases of lavender-water, and so on."† In all this effeminacy, betraying itself as it does even in the army in the field, cannot we see the influence of the corrupt ladies of society?

By their fault the gentleman of the Sword, scion of many a noble and famous stock, is no better than a veritable doll in women's hands. Those who have brought him to this state, wishing to keep him always in it, would cover him with ridicule, if ever he left off smiling; for indeed nothing could be more melancholy in this world of half-harlots, or to put it only too euphemistically, of half-virtue, than to see a painted face stripped of its gaiety and charm.

---

who was with the army, with regard to the operations of the campaign, and drawing a sort of plan for his use, had marked on the paper with *patches* the different places she advised him to attack or defend."—MME. DE GENLIS, *Souvenirs de Félicie,* Narrative of Mme. de Puisieux, mother-in-law of Marshal d'Estrées.

* MME. DE GENLIS, *Correspondance.*

† MICHELET, *Précis de l'histoire de France* (Abridgment of the History of France).

The *roués* were at first but actors formed by ladies of fashion, whose delight it was to perfect them in their part in a short series of lessons. Yielding to the demands of the most highly gifted among their in-structresses, gentlemen newly arrived at court, forced by circumstances to foreswear the old ideas of conduct that still survived here and there among provincial houses, soon learned to exaggerate their character of *mauvais sujet,* for they felt bound to hide as though it were something shameful the recollections they re-tained of childhood and early loves.

Some practices of the *roués* and men of pleasure who had as examples and patrons of debauchery first the Regent, later the hero of Port-Mahon and eventu-ally the notorious Marquis de Sade, display a peculiar character of erotic animosity very distinctive of their age, one in which physical gratifications were carried to the last degree of refinement. The artificial ardor in amorous pleasures of those days takes on a cynical form; not only does it boast of its excesses, but actually parades its abnormal indulgences with women, who again on their side make public profession of ingenious and far-sought refinement and corruptions.

In the eighteenth century simple vanity which wo-men turn each to her own profit as best she may, be-comes the sole and only motive of a sort of wild carni-val dance of sensuality. This same vanity under the constant exigencies of the sex, makes it the man of pleasure's unceasing task to be for ever in pursuit of "the fair," his flagging energies stimulated by the artificial aid of cantharides and similar aphrodisiacs, and accounts for the utter exhaustion of men of rank, and as a consequence the final shrinkage of the sword to almost a featherweight, even then seeming too heavy a burden for their breast to support.

The title of *seducers,* or lady-killers, a term invented in the last century by feminine cunning to describe men whom no woman could resist, is an expression at once offensive and inaccurate. Neither under the Regency, nor at any other period, have lady-killers really existed. The ancients attributed the characteristics of irresistible seduction to none but women. Male sirens were unknown to the ancient poets; the capricious nymphs they describe were always the aggressors, seducing the very gods themselves.

Is this to *seduce* a woman of so-called virtue, to master her some day, after she has definitely made up her mind to abandon herself to the most enterprising of a pack of fools,—who is to quit her side anon under the belief he is an irresistible conqueror of hearts? And by-the-bye, in this connection, what, think you, was the name Frenchwomen in 1780 gave to a timid lover? They called him "a German wooer."

Going no farther back than the vogue of the vigorous sensual type of Don Juan among women of fashion, there are found plenty of contemptible and self-satisfied asses to whom the daughters of Eve, in full enjoyment of their carnal attractions, were ready in mere *gaiety of heart* to offer the apple, bitten into already, and even sometimes not untainted with the venom of

the serpent. But the men who, in this world of corrupt morals, adopted in former days the bold part of
seducers, were not so in reality, in spite of their professed viciousness of life, their rouged and painted
cheeks and their costumes of slashed silk and velvet.
We cannot but recognize how insolent and how false
are the pretensions of these frail beauties when they
allege themselves victims of the fascinations of the professed Lovelaces, whose caresses, each duly counted and
recorded, great ladies competed for amongst themselves.
At this game, one in which their vanity was at least as
exacting as their senses, all knew quite well, that with
all their light way of taking a lover, they would have
to stomach some sorry tricks and shady practices on the
part of these men of pleasure, the experts and adepts
of love's mysteries. The coquettes of those days were
well aware what to expect in their intrigues, which
were deliberately premeditated, and the inconveniences
and perils of which they were familiar with before-
hand.

No! not even in France, a land where vice often
assumed exquisitely graceful forms, did *seducers,* veritable lady-killers, ever actually exist; but seductive
sirens there have always been found in plenty, eager to
pluck the delicate first fruits of young gallants of the
sword. For instance we may name the court-ladies
who besieged Louis XIV with their assaults, and that
long before his majority. These and their like, that
they might study after nature their artful manipula-
tions, proceedings which are now matter for the Crim-

inal Law, debauched young lads by force. At any rate it would appear so from the revelations of a certain amiable scamp of the fair sex, who very possibly was herself guilty of this kind of offence against good morals.

> Que fait-on de ces gueuses
> Qu'on mène à Chantilly?

(What do they do with the naughty baggages they take off to Chantilly?)

Under this description, at a slightly later date, were designated in a popular song of which the *avocat* Barbier quotes the words,* the most seductive ladies of the court. These elegant *kidnappers* of polite society used to pursue the young king Louis XV in the hopes of effecting his moral ruin.

---

* "It would appear they have not succeeded in the projected journey to Chantilly. The king thinks of nothing but the chase, and has no wish to try the. . . . I confess for my own part I think it a sad pity, for he is a well-built and handsome prince; but if his tastes are so, what can be done All the elaborate preparations of the women who thought they could debauch the king have given rise to the couplet of a popular song to the air of *Margot la Ravadeuse*, which runs as follows:

> Margot la Rôtisseuse
> Disait à son ami:
> "Que fait-on de ces gueuses
> Qu'on mène à Chantilly?" etc.

(Peg the Cookshop-keeper said to her beau, "What do they do with the naughty baggages they take off to Chantilly?") — BARBIER, avocat of the Parliament of Paris, *Chroniques de la Régence et du siècle de Louis XV* (Chronicles of the Regency and the Age of Louis XV), August, 1724.

Judging by the general behavior of the most fashion-able swordsmen and men of pleasure, it is plain how deeply, under the influence of women, the moral sense had been depraved among men of quality, and how they pursued without a prick of conscience a most despicable line of conduct.   The Maréchal de Saxe buys his equipment for the Army and his amusement there at the expense of the savings and the price of the jewelry of an actress.*   M. de Richelieu, whose ambi-tion is directed to procuring his king a supply of *ladies of extreme youth and some attractions,* borrows from one of his discarded mistresses a hundred thousand francs with which to cut a dash as ambassador at Vienna, proposing to undertake in that capital some diplomatic scheme or other of doubtful honesty.   Last, but not least disgraceful, a master of the arts of se-duction, a man of weak lungs, who is terrified at the sight of a spider,† the last of the Lauzuns, being really and truly in love with an Opera dancer, (he tells the story himself in his Memoirs), makes the chicken-hearted *protector* of the lady in question give him a thousand louis, and on these terms shares her favors with the paying lover.‡

---

* Adrienne Le Couvreur "had several persons much in her debt, amongst others the Comte de Saxe, to whom she had rendered great pecuniary services. . . ."—BARBIER, *Jour-nal*, March, 1730.

† DUC DE LAUZUN, *Mémoires*, Paris (Barroir), 1822.

‡ "One day he was for taking umbrage at her having spent the night with me and making a disturbance. . . . But as it might be advantageous to show some complaisance towards

Such principles, openly avowed by the leading *roués,* "men of the red heel at Versailles," representatives there of the old nobility of the Sword, give a sufficiently exact measure of the general honesty of their morals, dominated as these were by the charms of the sex. These bigwigs of elegant depravity, these fine gentlemen who, after their desperate bouts of erotic dissipation, sally out and play cock of the walk in the name of the mistresses they in their hearts despise, did not stop there. In 1726, Barbier declares in his *Journal,* the shameful vice, the vice against nature, comes again into fashion and prevails more extensively than ever. All our young lords, he says, were madly addicted to it, to the great chagrin of the court ladies.* Of these men thus brought to ruin and dishonor by their disgust for women, there were at that period in Paris alone, according to the police registers, something like forty thousand. After this nothing need surprise us.

Before Mesmer's magnetic tub, at sight of which they are fond of falling in a faint, the fantastic crea-

---

such a good man, he gave me a thousand louis, asked pardon for his ill temper, and agreed to Mlle. Tétard's keeping me on."—Duc de Lauzun, *Mémoires.*

* "The vice . . . has long been prevalent in this country, and for some time since has been more the fashion than ever. All the young lords were given up to it madly, to the great chagrin of the court ladies."—Barbier, *Journal,* May, 1725.

Under Louis XVI, according to the police registers, there were at Paris no less than 40,000 of these creatures. The figure is repeated by Bachaumont and Mercier. In Prussia, the number was yet more considerable.

tures of wanton pleasure, among whom are included some few of the highest rank and influence, henceforth ask for nothing else of deliberate purpose but super-natural excitements or profitable intrigues. In this way they endeavor to stifle their sensual regrets in eccentricities and distractions, sometimes merely odd, sometimes fraudulent. They speculate, swindle, cheat others or ruin themselves at cards. "The court is nothing better than a gambling hell,"* wrote Joseph II during his stay in France. The greatest ladies, follow-ing their *heart* more freely than ever, enter into rela-tions with the first comer. Then as a last refinement of debauchery they take to actors. Michu, Clairval, Jélyotte, had as many fine lady mistresses as they pleased. The most high-born of fashionable dames in-dulge in "merry doings" in the arbors of suburban inns, and enjoy the pleasures of low life at the tavern of Ramponeau. Some go in for free-masonry with Cagliostro, others for philosophy with d'Alembert, or give themselves up to acting, the stage indeed being their true element, and every one of them attracted by the glare of the foot-lights. The favored few play be-fore the Duc d'Orleans or at the theatre of Trianon, in the privacy of the royal circle, comedies and spectacles so indecent they could not possibly, says Bachaumont, be acted except before great princes or women of

---

* "The bankers at the queen's play-table, to obviate the cheating of the court ladies who trick them daily, have got leave from her Majesty to put certain precautions in force."— BACHAUMONT, *Mémoires*.

pleasure. From the repertoire of these may be mentioned, *Le Mariage sans curé*, *Léandre grosse*, *Léandre
étalon*, *l'Amant poussif*, and *Joconde*,* each more scandalous and abominably indecent than the other.

The Baronne d'Oberkirch relates how at the Castle
of Brunoy plays of such outrageous obscenity were
acted that no one could witness them without being
dishonored! "The fêtes as a rule terminated with *a
general orgy.*" Such are the details to be learned from
the gazettes and fashionable literature of the time with
regard to the conduct and morals of women, always
aided and abetted by the Sword.

Let us at this point analyze a little the complex influence thus invariably exercised over society by this
constant association of the two characters.

In these years of light-hearted joys and reckless vices,
when idleness is elevated into an actual and earnest
profession, men of quality wear out their energies in
doing nothing; they have just the needful time to de-
vote to their toilet. It is a matter of the first importance
to a man of pleasure to appear abroad only when powdered with proper art. "To be well dressed and appointed is sufficient alone to secure success, by making
us," one of the class has written, "popular with the
ladies; these are all-powerful and push us forward in
the world."

---

* Marriage without a Parson, Léandre with Child, Léandre
in the Stud, The Broken Winded Lover, Joconde, see HENRI
TAINE, *Origines de la France contemporaine*—L'Ancien
Régime.

Happy are the best powdered gallants, the *protégés* of ladies of a certain age and consequently of a higher degree of viciousness. These latter, following their well-known tendency that way, would engage in many a scandalous affair and shady intrigue, sometimes actually making traffic of younger women's favors. Their influence was very great, as it was they who introduced the king's mistresses to court, and associated with them in intimacy to please him.

At every age, and under all circumstances, the mass of women of luxurious life and wanton habits more and more incurs the contempt of men of quality. These last, careless of consequences and without any proper strength of character, appear henceforth to have abandoned, in weariness of spirit and weak selfishness of heart, all attempt to defend their matrimonial honor, so highly valued in former days. Profoundly convinced of the uselessness of their reproaches and the entire impossibility of constraining their dashing consorts to even a pretence of virtue, they grow utterly indifferent on the point, and as M. de Bezenval puts it, jealousy is now a thing of the past, even between lovers.

"When first I entered society," writes Cardinal de Bernis,* "I found it an established principle there that it was absurd for a husband to love his wife, or for a wife to love her husband."

"Any man who should wish to be the only one to enjoy his wife," says Montesquieu, "would be looked upon as a disturber of the public happiness." Accord-

---

* Cardinal DE BERNIS, *Mémoires.*

ingly the men of quality of this complaisant and cynical generation became as a rule, by a sort of perverted sympathy, the bosom friends of their mistresses', wives', or even their daughters' lovers.

In 1787, at Vienna no less than in Italy, noblemen allowed their wives a *cicisbeo* (or *friend of the house*), or even several such, the toleration of whom by the husband almost took rank as a recognized clause in marriage contracts. We can only repeat once more in this connection,—*Ce que femme veut, Dieu le veut.*

It was then a mark of good taste and breeding among the graceful *roués* of the period, *not* to be ticklish as to the honor of the ladies of the family, seeing such was their pleasure. The Regent himself had given the example of tolerance in this respect, an example followed in the neighboring courts.* Still, in spite of his lack of scruple in the matter of adultery and similar distractions with the fair sex, he opined, with regard to the point of honor, "that duels were really a trifle too old-fashioned." It is to the *Mémoires secrets* published under the pseudonym of Duclos that we are indebted for this curious detail.

After having masqueraded in women's clothes in pursuit of some naughty design,† as did the Abbé de

---

* The Margravine of Baireuth, sister of Frederick the Great, relates that during his stay at the court of Dresden he fell in love with the Princess Orselska, daughter of Augustus the Strong, who was at the same time his father's mistress, and that of his brother, Count Rutowski.—DR. JOHANNES SCHERR, *Society and Manners in Germany.*

† *La Vie de M. l'abbé de Choisy, de l'Académie franç.*

Choisy, not a few great noblemen marry beneath
them, a proceeding which among their proud ancestors
meant loss of rank. The Comte d'Evreux married the
daughter of a lackey who had made a fortune.*

Along with the battered survivors of the *roués* of
the Regency, most of them victims to the maladies in-
cidental to the indiscriminate Venus, the new generation, anemic and enfeebled, but ever bent on the pursuit of pleasure, after having followed lawless loves for
a while, veers suddenly to the pastoral, the idyllic, the
milk and watery. Its fêtes are enlivened by rustic
masquerades, flower-bedecked straw hats, shepherds'
crooks, while country dances are stepped to the sound
of tabors, tamborines and bag-pipes. Then it grows
grave, and plays at philanthropy. Again some devotees
of pleasure absurdly enough take up with revolutionary ideas, at once justifying and explaining the deli-
cious *bon mot* of Mme. de Lameth, who said, speaking
of her son who had turned *constitutionel*: "Why! I
must have passed a night, I suppose, in my anticham-
ber!" This is the time when, under the illusions fos-
tered by the *illuminati*, worn out debauchees dream
fondly (and this on the very eve of 1793) of purchas-
ing from the Comte de Saint-German the receipt for his

(Life of the Abbé de Choisy, Member of French Academy),
Lausanne, 1748.

* "Crozat married his daughter to the Comte d'Evreux, of
the noble house of Bouillon, who actually received fifteen or
sixteen hundred thousand livres as her dowry, but who never
slept nor lived with his wife, though a very amiable person."
—BARBIER, *Journal*, February, 1724.

famous elixir of life, that they may live indefinitely.

Meantime the different parts of Europe all endeavor to imitate French licence. Taking French fashions and above all French manners as models, their only thought is now, as ever, how to live after Parisian models.

Frenchwomen, an Englishman declares about the year 1785,* are the undisputed arbitresses of fashion, and this not merely in France, but in foreign countries, which all of them copy from France. They direct public opinion, and are thus the leaders in every vice. A French tourist wrote in 1787: "Our fashions and ideas are disseminated to the frontiers of Moldavia and Wallachia; from Pressburg to Cronstadt we give the tone to society."

For more than a hundred years now, the wives and daughters of Venetian nobles, the *gentildonne,* in open rivalry with the famous courtesans of that gay city, had "always imitated as much as possible French manners and fashions," as we read in the *Mercure de France,* a miscellany of the period. In Spain, the queen, to popularize French licence, "now and again indulged in the diversion of stripping naked along with her

---

* "In France it is women who dictate in a way what is to be said and prescribe what is to be done in the world of fashion."—JOHN ANDREWS, *A Comparative View,* 1785.

Saint-Cloud, August 6, 1722. "The Duke of Luxemburg's daughter, the Duchess de Rais, has plunged so deep in debauchery that, to gratify the Duc de Richelieu, she supped naked with him and his boon companions."—Princess PALA-TINE, *Letters.*

maids of honor, and then admitting to her apartments the best made men of the kingdom," so Voltaire relates in one of his letters.*

While the women of southern lands were thus imitating the corrupt morals of France, to west and east and above to northwards they grossly and coarsely exaggerated the vices of that country. At the very time when the Viennese ladies, and no less the citizens' wives of the same capital, indulged a similar spirit of dissipation, Catherine II was perverting her Russian fellowcountrywomen by the example of shameless licentiousness she offered them.

About the year 1772, the English ambassador, Lord Malmesbury, after speaking of German women as wanton harpies and noting the ill conduct of the sword at

---

* "We read in Voltaire's *Correspondance*: "I should be really glad for you to have known nothing of the news from Spain; in that case I should be enjoying the pleasure of informing you how the king of Spain has just had his wife, daughter of the late Duke of Orleans, put in confinement. In spite of her pointed nose and long face, she did not fail to follow the noble example set by her sisters. I have been assured that occasionally she enjoyed the distraction of stripping absolutely naked along with her prettiest maids of honor, and in this condition having the best-made gentlemen of the kingdom introduced into her apartments. The whole household has been broken up, and not a soul left in attendance on her in the castle where she is confined, but an old duenna. . . ."—VOLTAIRE, Letter to the Presidente de Bernières, dated July 20, 1724. Consult also the statement of Lemontey on *Les filles du Régent* in the *Revue rétrospective*, series I, vol. I, pp. 200-209, which confirms the particulars given by Voltaire.

that date, goes on, "At Berlin,—the same city which Frederick of Prussia used to designate a *filthy stable,* —no man is manly, no woman modest." "Every woman in the place has been ruined," wrote another observer of the same period, George Forster. Corruption indeed reached such a pitch that society ladies condescended to play the part of procuresses and debauch young girls. . . . Some of these ladies do not blush to sit in the theatre on the public courtesans' benches; while others indulge in orgies that would have astounded the Regent himself. These facts are recorded in the work of Dr. Scherr, where we may read much other evidence of Germanic demoralization, then at its height.

Beyond the Rhine, towards the end of the eighteenth century, "Officers' wives in especial are common prop-erty; their husbands sell, exchange and lend them to a comrade, each turn and turn about."* Lastly in Tur-key, where very soon the least worn-out *effendis* will not have more than one wife,† the harems had become hot-beds of depravity. Quite recently a high dig-nitary of the seraglio has pronounced the dictum, "The sultans of the present day are Frenchwomen."

It was under such conditions that European society reached its foulest and muddiest low-water mark, and which marks the end of the *ancien régime.*

This brings us to the sinister catastrophe of the

---

* Dr. JOHANNES SCHERR, *Society and Manners in Ger-many.*

† The Seraglio of Abdulrahman contained six thousand three hundred wives, concubines and black eunuchs.—GIB-BON, *Decline and Fall of the Roman Empire,* Vol. II.

drama. The sabre is now to replace the fine, straight blade of the nobler weapon,—the word *sabre* and *to sabre* only date from the end of the eighteenth century. The sword is a thing of the past! Duels are become exceedingly rare phenomena,* the Marquise de Nesle and the Comtesse de Polignac, rivals for the favor of a *roué* of limited resources, fought one with pistols† at this time. Yes! the sword is a thing of the past! The hysterical Théroigne de Méricourt (she was a Belgian from Liège), presently to be whipped, but always less than her deserts, by her friends the sans-culottes, will soon in the coming revolutionary days adopt as part of her decorative paraphernalia, in her role of *Citizeness General of Brigade,* the blade of uncouth shape that is to serve for the earliest assassinations of aristocrats.‡

The Sword is a thing of the past, and with it disappears finally anything resembling discipline. In June, 1789, "two companies of the *Gardes Françaises* refused to serve. Sent back to barracks, they break leave and are to be seen every evening, marching two and two down to the Palais Royal,—the general rendezvous of the light women whose lovers and hangers-

---

* "Nowadays the walking cane has replaced the sword, which is no longer worn habitually. ; ; ; The Parisian has voluntarily disarmed, for his own convenience and in the interests of common sense. Dueling was frequent; it has now become rare."—MERCIER, *Tableaux de Paris* (Pictures of Paris).

† RICHELIEU, *Mémoires.*

‡ H. TAINE, *L'Ancien Régime.*

on they are."*   During the sessions of the States General, sixteen thousand deserters used to prowl about the outlying parts of Paris, where they were lodged by prostitutes and other harpies, that have in all times been the agents of corruption for soldiers.

Such are the depths to which women and their wiles have at last degraded the nobility of the Sword.

---

* "Pretty near all the soldiers of the Guards belong to this class (of *souteneurs* or bullies), and indeed not a few enlist in the Regiment only to be enabled to live at the charge of these unfortunates."—PEUCHET, *Encyclopédie méthodique*, 1789, quoted by *Parent Duchâtelet*.—H. TAINE, *La Révolution*.

CHAPTER XV

LAST DAYS OF DEGRADATION—THE MAN OF PLEASURE—FINAL DISUSE OF THE SWORD

In these last days of the Sword, demoralized and debilitated as it is by excess, women of society, unused to fresh air and blanched by nocturnal indulgences, lose what is left to them of vigor, flesh and sexual zest. Their beauty of this later generation languishes, changes and deteriorates; no more do they display, as in Fragonard's *Chemise enlevée,* the charming, plump lines of the heyday of the Regency, the honeymoon, so to speak, of carnal pleasure.

Delicacy and sickliness, qualities that, speaking generally, are to dominate female charms henceforth, now come to be regarded as marks of distinction and high birth. The fair no longer answer to the type of perfect woman imaged by mythology and described by the poets of Greece.

This degeneracy of the female sex, which is before long to base its chief distinction on a native coldness of temperament, leads to a greater and ever greater enfeeblement of society, where "the hen crows louder than the cock."

In 1770 appeared a work entitled: *"Dégradation de l'espèce humaine par l'usage des corps à baleine* (Deterioration of the Human Species as a consequence of

the Use of Whalebone Corsets)*—a study demon-
strating the pernicious action of these articles. Incidentally, the makers of these terrible corsets, who were
men, tried them on ladies and girls with their own
hands.

Thus women of really sound health being from this
time on the exception rather than the rule, the process
of general deterioration makes giant strides. The man
of quality is a pale, withered looking creature, utterly
effeminated; for, more than ever now, do the ladies

---

* BONNAUD, *Dégradation de l'espèce humaine par l'usage
des corps à baleines, etc.* (Deterioration of the Human Species
as a Consequence of the Use of Whalebone Corsets, a Work
wherein it is proven to be against the Laws of Nature, to
further encourage the Depopulation of the Country and to
Debase Mankind,—to thus put it to the Torture from the
earliest Period of Existence, under the Specious Pretence of
training it to a Due Shape.)

"The public opinion of the century revolted *en masse*
against this fashion of corsets, one which the women would
not give up, however, at any price. It was a regular crusade,
from the remarks of *the modern Aretino* to the observations
of the anatomist Winslow, from the strong language of the
excellent Métra to the *Avis de Reisser sur les corps baleinés*
(A Word of Advice by Reisser on Whaleboned Corsets), and
the lamentations of the Chevalier de Jaucourt in the *Encyclopédie*. Throughout the century attacks on the article never
cease; it is held responsible for the death of a great number
of children,—responsible for the death of the Duchesse de
Mazarin. The form most in fashion was the *Greek* Corset,
first of all because of the name, and secondly owing to the
cheapness of the article, though this sort was very dangerous,
in as much as the whalebones only came up to the under part
of the breasts and might easily injure them."—E. and J. DE
GONCOURT.

make the chief merit of his puny person consist in certain special advantages, absurdly over-rated, such as good teeth, handsome eyes, white hands and above all fine legs, details which they themselves, if they have the smallest pretension to excel in them, are so fond of showing us.

Towards 1780, society ladies, tired of court abbés and philosophers, fishers in the troubled waters of revolution, phrase-mongers who are paving the way for the horrors of 1793, begin to weary of the high jinks of small and select supper-parties and of their "dear, delightful monsters." They set to work to change at their own good pleasure the particular forms indulgence is to take for the future. Unsettled in temperament, ideas and health, they put their heads together to find a remedy for the general disorganization and invent the "man of sensibility," the gentleman of quality in other words turned melancholic. Forever on the lookout for something novel and excessive in the way of sensation, they are fain to supplement vicious living by *sensibility*. After the open-hearted, frank obscenity, the mad dissipation, of an earlier day, they devise a new, exaggerated and complicated system of pleasure, a system of the head rather than of the heart, but which can still provoke in them a sort of bastard erethism. By these means they think to re-animate once more the senses whose zest they have well nigh annihilated.

Yet once again taking up the "pen of the ready writer," they make the man in the street their confidant, and reveal in letters and memoirs to the public at large and the mass of posterity, things that mere common decency should have made them hold their tongues about. Like Rousseau confessing his every baseness, they denominate this the *triumph of virtue.*

The fair dames of the period resorted to every means to stimulate their *sensibilities.* They seek excitement in dissecting dead bodies;* then again, after the perusal of Rousseau's *Emile,* they are frantic to mimic with ridiculously exaggerated affectations the transport of mothers' love, and in this way recommence their pernicious and debilitating influence over the rising generation, whose training they had systematically neglected for a long series of years.

In boudoirs still decorated with *amorini* and wanton pictures, which figured as a rule even in young unmarried girls' bedrooms, in face of representations of Priapus, god of gardens, of nymphs and naked satyrs, and emblems of love, fair dames and pretty maids, ever full of ingenious wiles, practice in the privacy of their chambers the rose-tinted magic of the new love. Adopting many an unexpected stratagem, they enter, by the road of pathos and angelic looks, on the new epoch when they will grant their favors only to the accom-

---

* "The young Comtesse de Coigny was so passionately fond of this dreadful study (Anatomy), that she would never start on a journey without taking in the boot of her traveling carriage a corpse to dissect, just as one takes with one a book to read."—Mme. de Genlis, *Mémoires,* vol. I.

This mania for dissection was for some time extremely fashionable with ladies of quality.

paniment of cries of horror and affright. A mass of
mannerism at the very instant of self-surrender, they
display their charms in an alluring confusion, and with
a grace that is the result of infinite study, and a quaint
combination of indecency and elegance. They are no
longer able under any circumstances to rouse, whether
for battle or duel, the old warlike enthusiasm of the
Sword; nay! by dint of their lamentations and tearful
sighs, they are rather a direct incentive to its progressive
enfeeblement.

They are for ever fainting,—in the theatre, in
church, at balls, in the streets, and above all in the arms
of their lovers, grown pretty callous by this time even
in the famous boudoirs with their alluring pictures.
However this new mode, this trick of theatrical
swoons,* with seductive little airs of confusion and
premeditated attitudes, did not last long. It is worthy
of note that the ladies, who weary so quickly of every
novelty, suppressed of a sudden and by common consent in 1821 the practice of these pretended seizures.

Be it observed at this point that it was solely in
self defence that the man of the Sword ever adopted
the ridiculous rôle of "a man of sensibility." He accepted the part only as a matter of necessity, because

---

* Among swooning ladies, one of the most seriously affected
was Mme. de Lamballe, whose case deserves mention. She
had fainting fits that frequently lasted for two hours; while
the scent of a bunch of violets was enough to make her ill,
and the sight of a lobster or crab, even merely represented in
a picture, brought on a nervous crisis.—MME. DE GENLIS,
Mémoires, vol. II.

now by the expenditure of a few fictitious tears, he was able to enjoy in a woman's arms the respite he so sorely needed.

Exhausted and in consequence liable to grievous chance of failure under the old rough and ready love-making, he welcomes with a readiness hardly complimentary to the sex, the repose the ladies, tired out themselves, are judicious enough to offer him.

To such *sentimental* relations of the Sword with the modern Heloïses did the absurd, insipid heroes of dark, hysterical mystery, who moulded themselves on Saint-Preux and Werther, owe their existence. On these ridiculous types was built up the whole school of impotent and despairing lovers, who under a nauseous pretence of being so romantic and interesting, prolonged for half a century longer the silly affectation of sentimental melancholy, in other words, a green-sickness of scepticism complicated with pulmonary consumption!

An adept in these last developments was bound under feminine guidance from 1785 onwards, to be ready to invoke nature on the smallest provocation, to understand the art of falling into sentimental rhapsodies at sight of the moon, holding sweet converse with a flower, a blade of grass, a star, calling heaven to witness or bursting into sobs on the shores of a lake. In this fashion did men of society, always under female guidance and impulse, succeed in bringing love itself into contempt at the end of the eighteenth century.

Simultaneously with this never-ceasing search for

pleasure, in Paris and in foreign lands alike, do the
proportions and vigor of the Sword everywhere show
manifest marks of degeneration. A familiar axiom of
economic science declares that "every vicious act is followed by diminution of force."

In Prussia the philosopher king, the flute-playing
monarch, Frederick II, seeing the stature of his Guards
and Grenadiers diminishing among the new recruits,
endeavored to get a set of taller men manufactured by
bringing together selected dames of stalwart physique
and soldiers of exceptional robustness of constitution;
but the results he obtained hardly came up to his ex-
pectations.*

In the eighteenth century there were very few
courtesans in the strict sense of the term. At that date
among *viveurs* it was at most a question of keeping
actresses, who would enter into a not very successful
competition with the ladies of the great world, their
comrades in dissipation at many a *souper fin*. Still
Maréchal de Richelieu used to protect girls of the
streets. "They were *more women* than the others,"
he used to declare.

---

* "He spared no expense or pains when it was a question
of getting big fellows for his Potsdam Guards. His recruiting agents hunted desperately after giants all the world over;
and he would pay from 1000 to 1500 thalers apiece for them.
The tallest of all, an Irishman, cost him as much as 1900. He
hoped to produce a race of drum-majors, by dint of marrying his fine soldiers to tall women, but the experiment did not
succeed."—DR. JOHANNES SCHERR, *Society and Manners in
Germany.*

In those days the professional light women were in matters of pleasure far less expert and consequently much less enticing than the ladies of society.

As for women of the middle classes, judging by the keen predilection for men of rank and soldiers they still exhibited at this period, it might be readily supposed, to use a phrase of a witty baggage of the time, that "they thought they were going to do the whole job themselves."*

The question of their virtue, which Retif de la Bre-

---

* Bassompierre tells us how women of the trading class would throw themselves at the head of men of rank: "For four or five months, it happened every time I passed over the Petit-Pont (at that time the Pont-Neuf was not built yet), that a pretty woman, a sempstress at the sign of the two Angels, used to make me deep curtsies, and would keep me in sight as long as ever she could. So soon as I noticed what she did, I used to look at her also, and return her bows with more carefulness. It came about one day that, on my arrival from Fontainebleau in Paris, passing over the Petit-Pont, as soon as ever she saw me coming, she put herself at the door of her shop, and said to me as I went by, "Sir; I am your very humble servant.' I returned her greeting, and turning round several times, I perceived that she followed me with her eyes as long as she could. . . . I then made my lackey dismount and give his horse to the postilion to lead, and sent him to tell her, that seeing the curiosity she showed to see and greet me, if she desired a more particular view, I offered to see her at any place she should name. She replied to the man that this was the best news any one could have brought her, and that she would go to any spot I preferred, provided it was on condition of sleeping between a pair of sheets with me. I accepted the arrangement."—Le Maréchal DE BASSOM-PIERRE, Journal de ma vie, Mémoires, June, 1606, edition by the Historical Society of France, vol. I.

tonne would hardly admit at all, brings us to quote the following passage from the Recollections of the Marquise de Créquy:

"The Major of the Gardes Françaises did not know whom to listen to and found it impossible to satisfy all the demands made upon him for the supply of sentinels and escorts,—Cartouche, it must be remembered, was at that time the terror of Paris. The Mousquetaires had begun by displaying a most laudable zeal, but it was soon discovered that these gentlemen were better at noise than real work. It was found that the security of merchandise might be bought too dear,—at the price of that of the merchants' pretty wives and the peace of mind of Parisian tradesmen in general, who soon wished all gay Mousquetaires to the devil!"

A very surprising result might be reached in the way of contrast, if reversing the actual facts of history, we should picture women doing exactly the opposite of what they have actually done. Just think what a different course the events of military history would have taken, if they had been left entirely unaffected by evil influences on the part of the sex. A single example chosen from modern times by way of striking proof will serve to embody and give actuality to this reflection.

If in 1868 a woman had not at Compiègne dissuaded the Emperor Napoleon III against accepting the alliance with Prussia, an alliance actually offered him by von Bismarck, we should have had no war of 1870. Without the war, we should have had no Commune

in 1871, and without the Commune we should not
have had the present republic, which is preparing the
apotheosis of noisy female politicians and intriguers,
wishing as it does to add them, as it will do some day,
to the electorate. Judging by such a series of consequences as here exhibited, we may realize what effects
have been regularly produced by women's intrigues in
the days when their authority was at its highest.

The pernicious influence they exercised stands revealed, we repeat the statement, at every stage of history; and their conduct in the past is a full and sufficient
explanation of every failure and every degradation the
Sword has had to undergo in the course of time.

"The deterioration of type among noble families,"
says Moreau de Tours, "is noted in numerous writers;
Pope remarks to Spencer on the sorry looks of members
of the English aristocracy in his day; and in the same
way physiologists had even earlier noted the short
stature of the Spanish grandees at the court of Philip
V." As for Frenchmen, long before 1789, they were
amongst the poorest specimens of humanity, according
to the testimony of many witnesses.

The Hindoos imagine that after the lapse of a certain cycle of years and attainment of certain degrees
of relative perfection, men pass into the form and condition of apes; accordingly these animals possess at
Benares a magnificent palace as their consecrated abode.
This curious belief is connected with a theory of Hindoo philosophy thus stated in the sacred books of the
Laws of Manu: "Man is made contemptible by wo-

men,"—a dictum that may very well serve to sum up our argument.

Even before the sword, the weapon *par excellence* of the gentleman, that had suffered so many gradual losses of size and weight according to the varying habits of different epochs, had been finally abandoned, the ladies of the great world had brought fashion into ut-ter and complete ridicule. The extravagance of their toilets, and particularly of their *coiffures,* passes the bounds of positive madness. Both sexes about 1780 are lavish and luxurious, but their luxury lies all in the direction of the mean and trashy. It displays itself in gauzy materials, and spangles and tinsel. Pleasure, now grown morbid and unhealthy, fails in zest, droops and languishes. Wit loses its *verve,* its fine ease and elegance, and the duel its correct and graceful conduct. *Courtesy,* already described by Richelet in his Diction-ary of 1680 as an "old fashioned word,"—courtesy, child of the fine old Gallic urbanity of an earlier age, is soon to disappear altogether. The English had seen and admired it at the Battle of Fontenoy; but they will look in vain for it,—the fact is notorious,—at Water-loo.

The forms of respect usual with women are now no more than a pretence. Ladies in general exact them only as a matter of etiquette; for in their eyes respect from a man implies contempt for their attractions or the idea that they are no longer young. There are of course sundry marks of deference prescribed by custom in the world of the drawing-room, where they are rigorously exacted, like the knot of ribbon, always the gift of a lady, which the *roués* used to carry attached to the sword-hilt. Generally speaking a custom survives the belief that originated; but though the form remains the same, the soul is gone.

Towards the end of the last century, before the assassinations of 1789 when one abominable fury actually devoured Major de Belsunce's heart (the atrocious act embodies a sort of allegory after all), the ladies of high life, as we have observed before, had by their own fault quite lost all consideration, and this not only in France but in other countries as well.

Now one last word as to the first and proudest ensign of nobility. After having weighed "fourteen pounds," like the sword of Alonzo de Cespède, "ten pounds, eight ounces," like the great Dietrich von Bern's (Theodoric's) broad-sword, "nine pounds, five Saxon *loth,*" like the blade of Conrad Schenk von Winterstetten,* or "five pounds, twenty-three ounces," like the brand of Scanderbeg, who would cleave a man bodily in twain, or according to a Crusaders' saying, "make two Arabs out of one,"—the sword, soul of primitive Gallic battle-frenzy, the sword, mother and queen of all other weapons, is everywhere abandoned.

---

* The sword of the Suabian Knight Conrad Schenk von Winterstetten, who died in 1242, weighed nine pounds, five Saxon *loth.*

On the blade are engraved the words: "Give this with my remembrance to the very worthy Conrad von Winterstetten, that noble heart; leave never a cap of mail entire."—F. A. FRENGEL, *Historical Museum at Dresden.*

It ceases to be an incarnation, a symbol; it ceases to exist in any true sense. The nobility of all countries, now fallen to utter decay, suddenly disarms of its own accord.

If overstepping the limit originally assigned to our subject, our analysis is extended half a century beyond the epoch when the Sword really ended its career, we shall find with the introduction of the flint-lock, the immediate successor of the old musket, the race of men and soldiers employing all their ingenuity to obviate the necessity of any laborious exertion of the human muscles.

Soon, succeeding generations, feeble and languid for want of sap and stamina, will see themselves reduced, in face of fresh engines of destruction, to yet further increase the range of distance at which battles are fought. Such is the effect of the continual advance made in scientific warfare by artificers, chemists, mechanicians, aëronauts and divers. In the near future, the great military powers will no longer be the nations that have the best generals and the bravest troops, or even the most approved artillery, but simply such as are able to buy from some new inventor means of destruction more deadly than all the others. This gives an element of disloyalty, a something underhand, to future battles. Personal prowess becomes of less and less importance.

Such in modern warfare is the inevitable and fatal tendency of human intelligence, making mere courage a decreasing factor in national life.

As to moral progress, looked at from the military point of view, can we say that, since the invention in Germany of the pistol in 1387; since the terrible artillery of Charles VIII, which scared all Italy before the battle of Fornova; since the employment of the stealthy torpedo—invented in 1771*—since the use, to come to later times, of rapid-firing arms of precision, of exploding shells, little favors of contemporary philanthropy ready to sacrifice its soldiers by tens of thousands, can we really say mankind has grown gentler and more humane in war? Is it enough to justify the high-sounding word, *Progress,* to nail up the Swiss red cross flag to a few wagons and call them ambulances?

No! there stand the figures to answer for us, and prove how the aforesaid progress maims and kills in battle far and away more of brave and efficient combatants, in proportion to the numbers engaged, than the most savage barbarism ever slaughtered.

In former days the wounds made by the sword, the *arme blanche,* were clean and healthy; Fleurange in one battle† received forty-six, and speedily recovered.

---

* Torpedoes were invented in America in 1771 by a certain Bushnell, who incurred such an amount of public odium that he was compelled to change his name and leave his country.

Subsequently they were brought to higher perfection by Fulton, the inventor of steamboats, and eventually tried in 1812 against the English fleet.

† "And subsequently was found the young adventurer (Fleurange) among the dead; who was not at first recognized, for he had forty-six very large wounds, whereof the smallest took six weeks to heal. And when his father had found

Finally, on actual inquiry into the general physical
condition of the soldiers of the present day, it is found
from the series of regulations governing conscription
in France and recent ministerial decisions on the subject* that in that country the average height of con-
scripts has fallen by an average of five centimetres
within the last sixty years alone. If we are to regard as
progress anatomical degeneration in men and enfeeblement of health and sexual power in women, a condition
of things that at the present day makes the latter by
common consent resort to drugs to promote their
occasional—and sterile—sexual enjoyments, may we
not more appropriately entitle all this a *progress of
degradation?*

M. Champouillon, Surgeon-in-Chief in the French
service, wrote not long since: "We are not justified

---

him, he put him on the horse of a camp-girl of *lansquenets*
who was found there; and so had him brought along with
the troops."—FLEURANGE, *Memoirs*, ch. XXXVII, year 1513.

* "We might be tempted to think the race of fine
men is disappearing, in view of the recent presidential deci-
sion which has just lowered the minimum of height fixed
for the *gendarmerie*.

"And observe, this is not the first time. Other previous
decisions had already reduced the said minimum of height
from 1 m. 71 to 1 m. 70 for the cavalry, and from 1 m. 69 to
1 m. 68 for the infantry.

"Well! it seems these concessions are not sufficient, and
the government, with despair in its heart, has just reduced
to this same figure last mentioned the minimum of height
required for *gendarmes*, but this time without any grace,
this stature being looked upon as indispensable *to impose
respect*."—*Figaro*, Dec. 17, 1878.

in counting upon the co-operation of the female to compensate for the present wear and tear of the male"*—hardly a reassuring opinon for the future of the race !

Happy days! when was seen taking part in a joust at Vienna a sturdy knight of a hundred summers;† happy days! when at the famous battle of Anghiari, of which Leonardo da Vinci was commissioned to make commemorative drawings, there fell on both sides, thanks to mail of proof, in four hours' fighting, only one man, and he was killed by a fall from his horse,

---

* M. Champouillon, Surgeon-in-Chief in the French Army, one of the chief ornaments of military hygiene in that country, has quite lately published a very interesting work on anemia, "that disease so essentially modern, and which has now long ago overpassed the limits of medical science to become a real and pressing social question." Dr. Champouillon treats it with equal knowledge and originality.

"A sight which has always struck me is this procession before the council of revision of the dry husks of the Parisian population, and notably of the class which the chronicles of the old tournaments represent as possessing the anatomy of giants. The greater part of these young people— I speak of those born and residing in Paris—are alike in showing a pitiful exterior, a frame long and slender, fragile as a stalk without any woody fibre, a pale complexion, colorless lips, a flaccid and transparent skin. To look at them, one would be tempted to say that death, when he comes, will find almost nothing left to destroy in them."

† In 1278 at a tourney which was held at Vienna, under the Emperor Rudolph I, a knight of a hundred years of age, Otto von Haslau, jousted with his great-grandson, Georg Turs. The fact is mentioned in S. MAILAITH, History of Austria, I.

as related by the Florentine Michiavelli in his *History of Florence*.

In days when fortifications were stormed at the point of the sword, regimental life was a liberal education for the rustic, and the profession of arms a patent of nobility to the veteran. The sword is a thing of the past, and for lack of it the old proud mien and the old punctilious sense of honor have ceased to exist in those classes where a fellow will first exchange the vilest epithets and foulest aspersions with his neighbor, and next minute go and clink glasses with him in the nearest tavern. Such degradation of character is found neither in Italy nor in Spain, countries of the *stiletto* and the *navaja* (knife).

There is no more to be said; the old world has lived its life, and dies of its inherent faults. The gentleman abandons the sword in sheer exhaustion, while dissipation, dying by inches of its own excess, reaches its last and final stage of degradation and decay.

The chivalric type of love endured for close upon five centuries; the spirit of genuine gallantry but two; cavalier ways and habits subsisted in their entirety barely sixty years; while finally the practices of the man of pleasure, the *libertine* modes, in full completeness, count at most only some forty years of life,—after which the reign of hypocrisy sets in.

Thus ends the Sword.

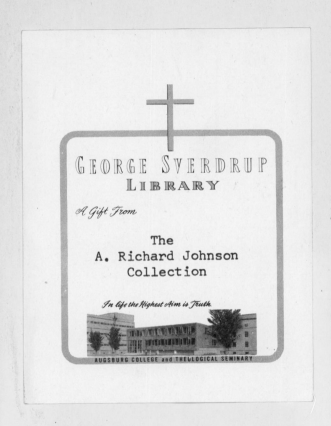